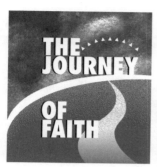

Called to
Radical Devotion

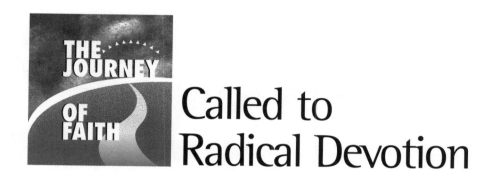

Called to
Radical Devotion

by David Morris

Charisma®
HOUSE
Books about Spirit-Led Living

CALLED TO RADICAL DEVOTION by David Morris
Published by Charisma House
A part of Strang Communications Company
600 Rinehart Road
Lake Mary, Florida 32746
www.charismahouse.com

Cover and interior design by Koechel Peterson

Library of Congress Card Number: 2001093781
International Standard Book Number: 0-88419-784-0

01 02 03 04 — 8 7 6 5 4 3 2 1
Printed in the United States of America

CONTENTS

CHAPTER ONE

Who We Worship

H IS HOME LIFE WHILE GROWING UP WAS LESS THAN IDEAL. Raised with an abusive, alcoholic father, an emotionally dependent mother and three siblings who either didn't care or were too preoccupied to offer help, Eric longed for the day he could be out of the house and free from the pressure he felt to be something other than himself. Though he thought he had found significance in a series of different relationships, it seemed a futile attempt to actually find love as each of them failed to provide what he needed. Amid the turmoil of personal pain and devastating circumstances, God showed up in Eric's life through a college friend who introduced him to the truth of Jesus Christ.

Eric immediately involved himself in this new church life and found it was the "home" he had always wanted and needed. The Bible studies were rich, as was the fellowship with other believers. Even times of worship were emotionally rewarding. Still, Eric had great difficulty connecting with God as his heavenly Father. Due to the abusive nature of his parental relationship, he felt he needed to keep God at a distance to remain safe. It was much easier to view God "out there" as someone whose input could be controlled. Sadly, it took quite some time for the healing process in his life to produce the fruit of understanding that God truly loved him just as he was.

Unfortunately, this is not an isolated incident. It is a very familiar story in the church. With many in this generation who have had absent or abusive fathers, one of the greatest needs is to experience a genuinely loving and caring father. Since one of the most prevalent needs in humankind is to be loved and accepted, a simple default human mechanism is for us to make God in OUR image and to reduce Him to our

IN THIS CHAPTER YOU WILL DISCOVER THAT...

▲ God truly is, and He can be known.

▲ God called Himself by names related to what He does for His people.

▲ God reveals Himself through His attributes.

▲ Jesus, God's Son, is truly God.

▲ Jesus is the foundation of Christianity.

deficient experiences with people. We begin to see Him as we do people, and we diminish the power of His greatness. We then often limit our expectations of God to how we would respond to those of lesser importance.

This makes me think of the parable of the master and the ten talents. (Read Matthew 25:14–30.) As you may remember, before departing on a long journey, the master entrusted three servants with his possessions. To the first he gave five talents, to the second two talents, and to the third one talent.

During his absence the first servant immediately invested the money wisely and gained twice as much. The second servant was just as smart as the first and did the same. But the third servant, the one who was given one talent, did something very strange, fearful and foolish. He dug a hole and buried the master's money.

When the master returned, he asked what the servants had done with his possessions. The first and second servants proved their loyalty by earning a significant amount of interest on their investment for the master, and they were commended with the words, "Well done." The third, however, confessed to burying the money and said, "Master, I knew you to be a hard man, reaping where you did not sow, and gathering where you scattered no seed. And I was afraid, and went away and hid your talent in the ground" (vv. 24–25).

How grim and unfortunate for this guy. The lazy servant had a preconceived idea of who the master was and how he would respond. Neither was accurate. Misunderstanding, misinformation and fear became the motivating forces behind his poor decision, and his ultimate fate became outer darkness.

At some point in time in our lives we must come to terms with the concept of God, who He is and what He wants. "Who is He… and what does He require?"

DO YOU REALLY UNDERSTAND WHO GOD IS?

The introduction to what is known as the "Doctrine of God" is that He IS, and He can be known! These two points establish the foundation and inspiration of true Christianity. The first is an affirmation of faith—believing that He truly is. The second is an affirmation of experience—believing that He desires to reveal Himself through personal relationship with His created beings.

God wants us to be informed about His personhood, His character, His love and His life. Many people today need a firmer grasp of God's intentions toward them before they are able to break down the barriers that separate them from His pleasure. This is the foundational role of worship. Worship is a natural instinct in each individual. We have been designed spiritually to give ourselves to the worship of something or someone, regardless of the seeming senselessness of how it may occur in our lives.

As elementary as this may sound, human beings *WILL* worship someone or something—either that which is beneath them or that which is above them. It is our destiny, as we were created for worship. One of the most fundamental concepts of worship is that the worshiper tends to become like his or her god.

Author Judson Cornwall says:

Those who have made a god of sex become lustful, indulgent people. The worshipers of sports become avid fans or participants in various sports events. History reveals cultures that worshiped a harsh, exacting cruel god and themselves became cruel and bloodthirsty people. Like it or not, we become like what we worship.[1]

Read Psalm 115:4–7. How does the psalmist describe the idols that have been made by the hands of men?

_____

_____

▲▲▲▲▲▲▲

Read Psalm 115:8. What happens to people who trust in the idols they made?

_____

_____

▲▲▲▲▲▲▲

> ▲ God wants us to
> ▲ be informed
> ▲ about His
> ▲ personhood, His
> ▲ character, His
> ▲ love and His life.

Read Romans 1:20–23. According to the apostle Paul, what happened to people when they rejected the knowledge of the true God to worship idols?

_____

_____

▲▲▲▲▲▲

Read Romans 1:28–32. What is the ultimate end for those who worship man-made idols?

_____

_____

▲▲▲▲▲▲

Historically, ancient civilizations have worshiped whatever they deemed worthy of attention, usually through fear and intimidation. The elements have long been worshiped as angry deities that must be appeased by their subjects through sacrifice and offering. The gods of rain, wind and fire are but the beginning of the great deception of *pantheism,* or worship of the earth. Still, take just one step beyond the temporal realm of what is seen, and find revealed the eternal realm of the Creator of those elements.

At its worst, *polytheism* (the worship of many gods) forces people to worship demons or other created things. At its best, it is simply an attempt to distribute the many characteristics of God to different hosts. These hosts do NOT desire a relationship with their worshipers. They merely demand obedience and loyalty. How dreadful to exist in a world of spiritual bondage where there is no mutual relationship between the worshiper and what is worshiped.

Read Psalm 96:4–6. How does the psalmist compare the true God with the idols of men?

_____

_____

▲▲▲▲▲▲

Read Psalm 97:7–9. What should be our response when we compare man-made idols with the power of God?

_____

_____

▲▲▲▲▲▲

Yet the world is full of people who are trapped in idolatry and have never come to understand who the true God is. Even the church has its share of people who believe they know God yet keep Him distant—because they really do not understand His nature. Still, from the very core of our being we cry out to be embraced by a genuinely interested, interactive and caring God. But due to pain and shame in our lives, we so easily gravitate to other things for worship satisfaction.

It is at that point where we must begin—with God alone. He is the reason for all things, the answer to the question of life and the object of our worship. He is not elusive. He can be known intimately!

Like Eric, many have come to believe in God through a series of difficult circumstances in life. Perhaps right now the Holy Spirit is creating a desire in you to go further into an honest relationship with God, one that supercedes that of a trivial churchgoer and introduces you to a whole new realm of reality—the reality of the actual presence of God.

PSALM 8:1–9, NIV

This psalm, written by King David, points out that even though God is full of heavenly majesty He also desires to know each of us intimately.

O Lord, our Lord,
  how majestic is your name in all the earth!

You have set your glory
  above the heavens.
From the lips of children and infants
  you have ordained praise
because of your enemies,
  to silence the foe and the avenger.

When I consider your heavens,
  the work of your fingers,
the moon and the stars,
  which you have set in place,
what is man that you are mindful of him,
  the son of man that you care for him?
You made him a little lower than the heavenly beings
  and crowned him with glory and honor.

> You made him ruler over the works of your hands;
>   you put everything under his feet:
> all flocks and herds,
>   and the beasts of the field,
> the birds of the air,
>   and the fish of the sea,
>   all that swim the paths of the seas.
>
> O Lᴏʀᴅ, our Lord,
>   how majestic is your name in all the earth!

YOU CAN KNOW THE LORD

Certainly the presence of God is incomprehensible. We as finite human beings cannot comprehend the infinite Being of God. His Being cannot be scientifically definable, nor can He be placed in the proverbial "box." The best humanity can do is define God's characteristics or attributes and leave His Being unexplained.

Read Acts 17:16. When the apostle Paul went to Greece to preach the gospel of Christ to the Gentiles, he became perturbed when he went into the city square in Athens. What was bothering him?

_____

_____

▲▲▲▲▲▲▲

Read Acts 17:24–28. Even though he was frustrated at the idolatry of the city, Paul stood before the people of Athens and told them about the true God. How did Paul describe Him?

_____

_____

▲▲▲▲▲▲▲

Paul introduced to the Athenians a radical concept: The true God wants people to seek Him—so they can find Him. God wants us to know Him! This truth is what sets Christianity apart from all other religions. Our God is a God of love who wants us to have an intimate relationship with Him!

If we are to know Him, however, we must understand His nature. There are two passages of Scripture that come close to a definition of His essential Being.

▲ "I AM WHO I AM" (Exod. 3:14).
▲ "God is spirit" (John 4:24).

God named Himself as "I AM" when He talked with Moses at the burning bush. He was intending to communicate that He could be no less than He is and needed to be no more. He is no other than Himself, and what He is, is enough. He always was and always will be—He is "I AM"! The power of God's name is just as powerful as God Himself.

> The concept of "name" is an important one in biblical worship. In fact, a synonym for "worship" in the Scriptures is the expression, "call upon the name of the Lord"… In biblical thought, a person's name encompasses his complete identity, reputation and character and refers to his whole self or person.[2]

Throughout the Old Covenant God revealed Himself to Israel by bailing them out of bad situations. The names by which He called Himself were directly related to what He did for His people at certain times in their history. The compound names of God are descriptive of the revelation of His character that was crucial for the moment:

▲ *Jehovah Jireh*—The Lord who provides (Gen. 22:14)
▲ *Jehovah Rapha*—The Lord our healer (Exod. 15:26)
▲ *Jehovah Nissi*—The Lord our banner (Exod. 17:15)
▲ *Jehovah M'Kaddesh*—The Lord who makes you holy (Exod. 31:13)
▲ *Jehovah Shalom*—The Lord our peace (Judg. 6:24)
▲ *Jehovah Rohi*—The Lord our shepherd (Ps. 23:1)
▲ *Jehovah Tsidkenu*—The Lord our righteousness (Jer. 23:6)
▲ *Jehovah Shammah*—The Lord who is there (Ezek. 48:35)

The Bible never operates with an abstract concept of God, but it describes Him as a living God who enters into relationship with His creation. As "Spirit," this means He is the breath, the

---

And Abraham called the name of that place The LORD Will Provide.
—Genesis 22:14

I, the LORD, am your healer.
—Exodus 15:26

And Moses built an altar, and named it The LORD is My Banner.
—Exodus 17:15

I am the LORD, who makes you holy.
—Exodus 31:13, NIV

Then Gideon built an altar there to the LORD and named it The LORD is Peace.
—Judges 6:24

The LORD is my shepherd, I shall not want.
—Psalm 23:1

And this is His name by which He will be called, "The LORD our righteousness."
—Jeremiah 23:6

And the name of the city from that day shall be, "The LORD is there."
—Ezekiel 48:35

true essence and the originator of all life. Though He cannot be seen with human eyes, He is nonetheless very real.

So, to begin our journey toward the true worship of God, this question must be asked: What makes our God so unique and different from all others and worthy of allegiance and loyalty?

Most religions have components that include a deity, pre-scribed methods of service and rules that must be followed in order to obtain accessibility to this deity, thereby attaining a "higher state of awareness." If loyal, one can expect certain benefits. It usually goes like this: "If you're good, then you are rewarded. If you're bad, then you are reprimanded." But none have the relationship factor that combines the blessing of life through intimacy with their Creator, as does Christianity. The true God has chosen to reveal Himself to His creation.

▲▲▲▲▲▲▲▲▲▲▲▲▲▲▲▲▲▲▲▲▲▲▲▲▲▲▲▲▲▲▲▲▲▲▲

What makes our God so unique and different from all others and worthy of allegiance and loyalty?

▲▲▲▲▲▲▲▲▲▲▲▲▲▲▲▲▲▲▲▲▲▲▲▲▲▲▲▲▲▲▲▲▲▲▲

Our God allows and honestly desires that unique blend of obedience and faith birthed from a genuine encounter with Him that leads to a developing relationship. Establishing an intimate relationship with His people has been His quest from the begin-ning of time. Through sin, we've fallen from God's intended harmonious connection to Him. But that was reclaimed through Jesus' sacrifice on the cross and can be personally experienced as we pursue and receive revelation of His heart's desire for us.

HOLY, HOLY, HOLY

This great hymn was written by an English poet and clergyman John B. Dykes (1783–1826), who served as an Anglican bishop in India. He wrote fifty other hymns, including "From Greenland's Icy Mountains."

Holy, holy, holy, Lord God Almighty!
Early in the morning our song shall rise to Thee;
Holy, holy, holy, merciful and mighty!
God in three Persons, blessed Trinity.[3]

THE ATTRIBUTES OF GOD

Besides revealing Himself through the nature of creation and by the internal human conscience, God is revealed by His attributes or characteristics. They cannot be separated from Him, as they are not *part* of Him, but rather are God Himself. Although we will use it, the term *attributes* is not completely accurate since by definition it connotes something added to the divine Being called "God." The terms *perfections* or *virtues* would communicate better. Still, most understand the use of the term *attributes*. The only reliable knowledge of these attributes is found in the Scriptures.

With that in mind, a basic ingredient to approaching the concept of God is always to remember that He is "transcendent" and "immanent." That is—He is both the magnificent Lord of the universe and the tender Lord of our lives, nearer than the very breath we breathe. He is both great in power and humble in heart. His immensity or vastness emphasizes His transcendence, and His omnipresence emphasizes His immanence or closeness.

Let's look at several of the attributes of God more carefully.

1. God is holy.

Jehovah God, as He is known from the Old Testament, is holy. Though in our culture this attribute may seem rather obtrusive and unapproachable, He informs us that because He is holy, we can actually be holy also.

Read 1 Samuel 2:2. How did Hannah, the mother of Samuel, describe God?

_____

_____

▲▲▲▲▲▲▲

Read Leviticus 20:7–8. What did the Lord tell Moses He would do for the people?

_____

_____

▲▲▲▲▲▲▲

We see that even though there is no one as holy as the Lord, He has made a way for us to share in His holiness. This He ultimately accomplished through the sacrifice of His Son, Jesus Christ. The purpose of sending Jesus was to have a union of fellowship with us—divinity and humanity as companions.

One aspect of the holiness of God is depicted through the burning bush as He spoke to Moses. This is the first time God is recorded as using a vehicle for conversation. (You can imagine what Moses may have thought.) God told him to remove the sandals from his feet because the ground on which he was standing was holy (Exod. 3:5). Unlike the culture of our day where men remove their hats out of respect, the sandal removal in that day was to prove uncleanness and unworthiness in the presence of someone so distinctly holy, pure, clean and sacred.

God's holiness is also displayed and revealed in the moral law that is implanted in man's heart and speaks through the conscience. The impossibility of keeping God's complex moral law was to prove to His people that He alone was holy and that the highest revelation of that law would one day come through the man Jesus Christ.

A definition that many scholars adhere to with regard to the uniqueness of God's holiness is that He is wholly "other." That is to say, He is completely different from any other god. There is no comparison to His eminence, distinction, prominence, importance, reputation or renown. He is absolutely distinct from all creation and is exalted above everything in boundless majesty.

2. God is infinite, eternal and perfect.

God is infinite and eternal. He dwells in a state of being absolutely perfect, where He is elevated above all temporal limits regarding time and space. He possesses the whole of existence in one indivisible present. God's essence qualifies all His attributes. He is infinite in His knowledge and wisdom, in His goodness and love, in His sovereignty and power. All His perfections are free from limitations and defects.

God did not have a beginning, and He will never end. He will never change, either. He will not get old, wear out or lose His power.

> Then He said, "Do not come near here; remove your sandals from your feet, for the place on which you are standing is holy ground."
> —Exodus 3:5

Read Psalm 31:1–3. In Old Testament language, the psalmists described God as "a Rock" because of His eternal, changeless nature. How did it make David feel when he thought about God being his "Rock"?

_____

_____

▲▲▲▲▲▲▲

How did David expect God, as his "Rock," to help him?

_____

_____

▲▲▲▲▲▲▲

3. God is almighty.

Though many throughout history have claimed to serve great gods, none have proven to be almighty. Our God is omnipotent. That means He is all ruling, all-powerful and can do anything as the absolute and universal sovereign. He is the One who spun worlds into existence, creating galaxies and universes far beyond what we can comprehend. He is the One who birthed the earth by the words of His mouth and fashioned everything in it simply for His pleasure.

And He is the one who will ultimately judge the world at the end of time. He is in complete control of the universe He created, and He will have the ultimate say over its destiny.

4. God is omniscient.

He knows everything there is to know because it is intrinsic within His nature. He has no need to venture outside Himself to learn a thing—past, present or future. All knowledge, understanding and wisdom are inherent within His Being. He created every insect, every bird, every snowflake, every grain of sand, every precious stone hidden in the ground and every weather pattern in the atmosphere. He also knows our thoughts and motives, and He knows how many hairs are on our heads.

Read Psalm 139:13–16. How well does God know us?

_____

_____

▲▲▲▲▲▲▲

5. God is righteous and just.

He is equitable in character, in word and in deed. He can never lie. Everything He does is done right and in a flawless manner. There can be no accusation against His integrity because He is perfect! Justice says He must render to all what they deserve. When man sinned, God's only recourse was to ban man from the Garden of Eden, where God's perfection was manifested in the tree of the knowledge of good and evil.

God is the most righteous judge on earth—because He is capable of extending mercy without compromising His standards of righteousness.

Read Psalm 145:17–19. How did the psalmist describe the righteousness of God?

_____

_____

▲▲▲▲▲▲▲

6. God is faithful.

He is trustworthy, sure and truthful. He will be true to us until the end—as in a marriage covenant. In fact, in the Bible God often compares His loving commitment to us as a wedding vow. He is faithful to Himself and faithful to His people, because He sees things as they really are and knows the end from the beginning.

Read 2 Timothy 2:13. What happens when we are not faithful to God?

_____

_____

▲▲▲▲▲▲▲

7. God is good.

He is filled with grace, mercy and patience. He is the source of all good things creation enjoys, dealing bountifully and kindly with all. In fact, He showers His blessings every day on people who do not worship Him or acknowledge His existence. He extends His love and favor to people who never thank Him or acknowledge Him.

Read Matthew 5:44–45. What did Jesus say about the Father's goodness toward sinners?

_____

_____

▲▲▲▲▲▲▲

8. God is love.

First John 4:8 says plainly that "God is love." Love is His essence. He cannot do anything apart from love. His goodness is demonstrated because of His love—the aspect of His essence that motivates Him to communicate consistently. He loves because that's who He is, and He is always drawing humankind to Himself, the originator of love.

9. God is worthy.

He is competent, ample, fit and entirely deserving of all praise, worship, honor and undying devotion (Rev. 5:9)! Because He created all things, and by His blood redeemed all things, He alone is worthy to take the throne as Lord of all!

We find in the Scriptures that Jesus, who is the Christ or "The Anointed One," is the express image of the Father (Col. 1:15). When asked by the disciple Philip, "Lord, show us the Father," Jesus said to him, "He who has seen Me has seen the Father" (John 14:8–9). Jesus is what God looks like if He had skin!

YOU ARE LORD OF HEAVEN

I wrote this song a few years ago to extol the majesty of God. Choruses like this have the power to lift our spirits and focus our attention on His greatness.

> You are the Lord of heaven,
> And the Lord of earth,
> You are Lord of creation, the universe;
> The earth is the Lord's
> And the fullness thereof.

And they sang a new song, saying, "Worthy art Thou to take the book, and to break its seals; for Thou wast slain, and didst purchase for God with Thy blood men from every tribe and tongue and people and nation."
—Revelation 5:9

And He is the image of the invisible God, the first-born of all creation.
—Colossians 1:15

Your mercy is without end,
Your power without measure;
And holiness establishes Your throne.

You are Lord, Jehovah the Lord our God
You are Lord, El Shaddai, Almighty One.
Your ways are forever and ever the same.

Your kingdom is without end,
Dominion without measure
And righteousness, the scepter of Your throne.[4]

THE REVELATION OF THE SON OF GOD

Many people have imagined God to look like the old man who portrays Father Time—with a long, flowing beard, a toga wrapped around his chest and holding a staff. Actually, if Jesus resembles that guy, then God looks like that. The Bible says, "No one has beheld God at any time" (1 John 4:12). But now, through Jesus, we can behold the glory of the Father.

Read Hebrews 1:1–2. The writer of Hebrews tells us that in times past God spoke through the prophets. Now, in these latter days, how does God reveal Himself?

_____

_____

▲▲▲▲▲▲▲

God came to earth in human flesh so we could more comfortably relate to Him and so He could relate to us through what Jesus experienced on the earth. He is "one who has been tempted in all things as we are" (Heb. 4:15).

Identifying Jesus as the Son of God is the most important revelation that has graced this planet. If we are to become true worshipers, we must understand who Jesus is!

A conversation between Jesus and His disciple Peter may be one of the most famous in the entire Bible. Jesus asks, "Who do people say that the Son of Man is?" (Matt. 16:13). His disciples answered, "Some say John the Baptist; and others, Elijah; but still others, Jeremiah, or one of the prophets" (v. 14). Then Jesus asked again, "But who do you say that I am?" (v. 15).

▲▲

Identifying Jesus as the Son of God is the most important revelation that has graced this planet.

▲▲

Since the beginning of the New Covenant Age, Peter's answer has been the cornerstone of the Christian faith: "Thou art the Christ, the Son of the living God" (v. 16). Peter recognized Jesus as the "Messiah," "The Anointed One," "The Chosen One" and "The One who comes in the name of the Lord." Jesus then pronounced a blessing on Peter by acknowledging that "flesh and blood did not reveal this to you, but My Father who is in heaven" (v. 17).

For all practical purposes, this is the foundation of Christianity. Jesus said He would build His church upon the rock of this confession and the gates of Hades would not overpower it (v. 18).

The people in the first century asked the question, "Who is this man?" What Jesus did in the lives of His contemporaries caused numerous questions to arise. Where did He come from? What was His purpose? Was God actually His Father? Was He really who He said He was?

Philosophers and cynics have asserted that Jesus was simply a fable propagated by fanatics throughout the centuries of time. They view the claim of His resurrection from the dead as a myth passed down from generation to generation. Some have said that Jesus was only a man made into a god by centuries of evolving Christian theology. However, around A.D. 112, the ancient historian and Roman administrator Pliny the Younger recorded that very early in Christian history His followers worshiped Him as Lord.

Besides the Bible, there are numerous concurring accounts from first-century writers affirming that Jesus was a real person who lived, died and was believed to have been resurrected. To counteract the common claim that Jesus was a product of Christian imagination, early non-Christian writers

> Upon this rock I will build My church; and the gates of Hades shall not overpower it.
> —Matthew 16:18

have clearly stated that His followers viewed Him as divine from the beginning.

Clement, the leader of the church at Rome in A.D. 95 (about the same time the New Testament was completed), wrote to the Corinthian church. In this letter he distinctly sets forth the divinity of Jesus and anchors the authority of the gospel to the resurrection, arguing strongly that Jesus is Lord and God!

Justin the Martyr, Clement of Rome, Ignatius and other writers such as Quadratus and Barnabas stand united against the accusation that Jesus was "invented" by the church over centuries of its history. The simple facts refute this charge completely. And so if we had no New Testament, on the basis of extra-biblical and historical evidence we can know that:

▲ Jesus Christ existed in history.
▲ He was crucified by Pontius Pilate.
▲ The first Christians believed Him to be raised from the dead.
▲ The early church worshiped Him as Lord.
▲ Jewish opponents tried to slander Him, but never denied His existence.

The facts of Christian faith were settled early in church history and are in no sense the invention of later revisionists.[5]

So if Jesus really existed and said He was God, there's no way He could be accepted as a prophet or a "Good Teacher" and disregarded as deity. He declared that He was divine. Could a good teacher or a prophet who spoke in the name of the Lord make such a claim, yet be lying and still be considered a reputable source of truth? That would negate His ability to speak in the name of the Lord. He is who He said He is.

The question "Who do you say that I am?" still rings out through the ages and requires a response. An essential element of biblical and historical truth that demands attention is identifying who Jesus is! This, to me, is the beginning to understanding concepts of worship. We must answer the question!

BEHOLD YOUR GOD

First, the revelation of who He is must penetrate the depths of a humanistic, hardened heart that chooses to shut out truth due to a lack of understanding, the pain of life or bad religious experiences. Reckoning with the living God is all encompassing when He is truly seen. We have all seen Him hanging on a cross, suffering and dying. But many have not fully realized that He is no longer there. The fact that He has risen proves His divine nature has overcome all human powers, defying the simple laws of nature.

It would be difficult to try and separate who Jesus is from what He did. This is the One whom the Holy Spirit conceived in Mary's virgin womb, the One born in a stable in Bethlehem. This is the young boy who taught in the temple in Jerusalem, confounding the religious scholars of the day. He's the same boy who grew up in a carpenter's shop, learning the trade of Joseph, His earthly father. After being baptized by John, the Holy Spirit descended upon Him, as a voice from heaven was heard saying, "This is My beloved Son, in whom I am well-pleased" (Matt. 3:17). It is He who called twelve men to serve as His disciples and associates, and these twelve watched Him heal the sick, raise the dead and preach the good news of the kingdom of God.

This is the One who was betrayed by a friend, died the death of a cursed man upon a Roman cross while carrying the weight of mankind's sin. He was buried in a borrowed tomb. Yes—the same One who rose from the dead on the third day, ascended into heaven and now sits at the right hand of the Father, interceding for us!

Not only did Jesus reveal the Father to us, He is also our access to the Father. Jesus did not ascend to heaven to secure our salvation—that was done on Calvary. He ascended to secure permanent access to the Father that we might become worshipers!

Read Ephesians 2:18. How did the apostle Paul say we come to the Father?

_____

_____

▲▲▲▲▲▲▲

Read John 14:6. How did Jesus Himself say we could approach God?

_____

_____

▲▲▲▲▲▲▲

It is not possible to come to God by any other means than through His Son. Our current culture tells us there are many ways to "enlightenment." *Enlightenment* is a sort of "code" word, meaning to imply that one can find God, inner peace and the meaning of life through a variety of sources. The world would want us to believe that whatever makes you happy, whatever floats your boat, whatever turns you on leads to God—not true!

So who do *you* say Jesus is? Is He just a familiar name from the pages of an ancient book? Is *Jesus* simply a word you hear being used on the streets and at the office by people who have no understanding or regard for the eternal realm? Is He your friend, or perhaps your buddy? Is He a Father, a business associate, a peer, a brother... a lover? What is the depth of relationship you have with Him? How intimate are you? Whatever your present relationship is with the King of the universe, it's bound to get better as you discover a deeper understanding of His ways and receive fresh revelation about His Being.

> So who do *you* say Jesus is?

In a heavenly vision, the apostle John received revelation and saw the Lord. (Read the Book of Revelation.) Likewise, Isaiah, Ezekiel and Daniel did also. (Read Isaiah 6; Ezekiel 1; Daniel 7–8.) Each had a vision of a holy place in a temple, a throne and of some phenomenon surrounding or proceeding from the initial vision experience. John saw a Lamb in the center of the throne. Isaiah saw the Lord on the throne with great glory and an altar with coals of fire. Ezekiel saw the Lord shining like burnished bronze on a throne resembling a bright blue stone. And Daniel saw "the Son of Man" coming up to the Ancient of Days, who was seated on the throne in the presence of thousands upon thousands. In each case, the overwhelming splendor of the encounter caused the onlooker to fall down before the throne and worship. These men were eternally awestruck with what they saw in the realm of heaven's glory.

Looking at Jesus in the Book of Revelation shows a transcended state of His original character from the Gospels. This Book of Revelation to John is the paramount worship book of the New Testament. With literary imagery and symbolism from the Old Testament, the final drama of Christ's victory was written in letter format to the seven churches of ancient Turkey. Knowing John and the language of the day, the first-century church had cultural and ethical interpretations of the poetic and prophetic implications in this letter. As well, they had understanding regarding the descriptive worship of the Lord God and the Lamb.

Read Revelation 1:17. How did John respond when he saw the Son of God in His heavenly glory?

_____

_____

▲▲▲▲▲▲▲

From its beginning, the Book of Revelation is a worship experience. The focal point is what transpires around and from the throne of God. Heaven looked like a busy place to John. Besides God on the throne, he described creatures, elders, more thrones and thousands upon thousands of people, glory, awe and splendor. Sounds like nothing short of total sensory overload!

In the fourth chapter, songs of worship are ascending to Him who sits upon the throne. Chapter 5 brings the slain Lamb into view, then exalts Him as the One who redeemed all men to God. He then becomes the central theme of John's message and the object of each worship expression. Jesus becomes the understated entity, worthy to receive all glory, honor and praise.

Jesus is the proper object of our worship, for He Himself is in the Father. He taught that clearly when He said, "Believe Me that I am in the Father, and the Father in Me" (John 14:11). Even while on earth, Jesus received worship. At His birth, the angels and the shepherds worshiped Him. And during His ministry He received worship from a ruler, a leper, Mary (after the Resurrection), the disciples and others. Certainly He would not have allowed them to worship Him if He were not worthy to receive it.

Judson Cornwall relates it this way: "In accepting worship, Jesus Christ was admitting and declaring Himself to be God; therefore, He is totally worthy of all worship."[6] In heaven, the saints and angels bow in worship. And the Word says that every knee will bow (in worship) and every tongue confess that Jesus Christ is Lord, which will bring glory to the Father (Phil. 2:10–11).

▲▲▲

True worship is birthed from an encounter with God's holiness. He is worthy because of who He is!

▲▲▲

The Scriptures teach that our worship is to God in the name of the Lord Jesus. We give thanks through Him to God the Father (Col. 3:17). Most of our common worship expressions are of Jesus or in His name. Even our liturgies and worship formats are in remembrance of Jesus. So regardless of whether we worship the Father through the Son or worship the Son in the Father, the depth of our expressions are based on our personal concepts of the One we worship. If we don't see Jesus as God, we will not give Him the respect due Him.

The people who interacted in the life and ministry of the Lord saw Him in various lights. The roles He assumed in people's minds were essentially based on what He could do for them. To some He was the Healer, the Savior or the Comforter. To others He was the One who

That at the name of Jesus every knee should bow, of those who are in heaven, and on earth, and under the earth, and that every tongue should confess that Jesus Christ is Lord, to the glory of God the Father.
—Philippians 2:10-11

And whatever you do in word or deed, do all in the name of the Lord Jesus, giving thanks through Him to God the Father.
—Colossians 3:17

would deliver them from Roman tyranny as an earthly king. While these are facets of His personhood, supported by what He did and how He impressed them, the New Testament does not declare Him specifically to be any of these things. The only consistent message of Jesus' role is that of LORD!

Do we worship God simply because He is, or because of what He can do for us? When He makes His presence known, do we work Him or worship Him? Appreciation for His great deeds evokes genuine praise. But true worship is birthed from an encounter with His holiness. That is the element that strips us of our self-awareness, self-consciousness and self-absorption and creates an authentic hunger for His glory—that which cannot be satisfied by anything trivial in life.

LET'S TALK ABOUT IT

▲ Many Christians picture God as a stern, angry judge who is seated in heaven, always ready to punish us whenever we sin. How does such a warped concept of God prevent us from having a close relationship with our heavenly Father?

_____

_____

▲▲▲▲▲▲▲

▲ Look at the different attributes of God that were described in this chapter: holy, infinite, almighty, omniscient, righteous, just, faithful, good, loving and worthy. Do you struggle with believing that God has these qualities? If so, which ones? Why is it hard for you to accept the fact that God is like this?

_____

_____

▲▲▲▲▲▲▲

▲ Why is it so important for us to believe that Jesus Christ is more than a good teacher, a great philosopher or a moral leader?

_____

_____

▲▲▲▲▲▲▲

▲ The Book of Revelation gives many visual images of worship in heaven. How do you think we are supposed to re-create this kind of worship on earth?

_____

_____

▲▲▲▲▲▲▲

YOUR TIME WITH GOD

As you contemplate what you have learned of the attributes of God from this chapter and upon your own worship of Him, spend time alone with Him, praying these words:

Father, I pray that Your Holy Spirit would open my eyes so that I can understand who You really are. Strip away the wrong concepts I have of You. I want to know Your goodness, Your mercy, Your holiness, Your righteousness, Your justice, Your faithfulness, Your almighty power and Your everlasting love.

Please open my eyes so that I may behold You in Your glory. Let me see You as the apostle John saw You when he was on the island of Patmos. Pour out on me the spirit of wisdom and revelation that I might see Jesus Christ as the only Son of God—the Lamb of God who was sacrificed for my sins and for the sins of the whole world.

I choose to make Jesus the focus of all my worship, because He alone is worthy of my praise and devotion. I will not worship any other gods or fashion any idols that steal my attention away from Him. Make me a true lover of Christ. Amen.

CHAPTER TWO

The Father Is Seeking Worshipers

IN THIS CHAPTER YOU WILL DISCOVER THAT GOD...

▲ Created man to have fellowship and communion with Him.

▲ Is seeking worshipers—not worship.

▲ Will transform your life through an act of worship.

IT WAS A HOT DAY ON THE DUSTY ROAD TO GALILEE. Weary from the journey, Jesus decided to stop in the city of Sychar in Samaria around suppertime. His disciples had gone into the city to buy food and had left Him alone. He found a place to rest by one of Jacob's centuries-old wells. Not long after He sat down to rest, a Samaritan woman came to the well to draw water, and Jesus asked her for a drink. Surprised by His seeming familiarity, she said, "How is it that You, being a Jew, ask me for a drink since I am a Samaritan woman?" (In those days, Jews had no dealings with the Samaritans. In fact, the Jews considered them half-breed dogs!)

In response to her, Jesus said, "If you knew the gift of God, and who it is who says to you, 'Give Me a drink,' you would have asked Him, and He would have given you living water" (John 4:10). Herein lies the famous story about the well of living water springing up into eternal life, which is salvation. In addition, this is probably the most famous passage on worship in the Bible.

The interchange between this Samaritan woman and Jesus is nothing less than amazing. Imagine this poignant scene as Jesus creates an historical reference point for centuries to come.

First of all, it was not customary for men to speak to women in public. Nor was it common for Jews and Samaritans to interact. But this interesting concept, which recurs in Scripture, is reiterated in the life and ministry of Jesus. The initiation of conversation begins with the Lord Himself. He asks for something of natural value in exchange for something supernatural. In essence, He asks for the woman to open the door so He can have fellowship with her.

GOD'S RELATIONSHIPS WITH MAN

The idea of relationship was in the heart of God from the dawn of time. In fact, the earliest parts of the Bible are filled with stories of God's relationship with the people who worshiped Him.

Adam and Eve

Adam and Eve were created in the image of God and were engaged in relationship with God from the beginning. That's what they were created for—to have fellowship and communion with God. After Adam and Eve fell into sin, God's heart toward humankind never wavered. He remembered the times when He would walk with Adam in the cool of the day. He recalled that their fellowship was sweet. He still desired relationship and set a course to redeem mankind back to Himself. God's first recorded words after the Fall were to Adam: "Where are you?" (Gen. 3:9).

Enoch

Enoch, Noah's great-grandfather, was so in tune with God in his generation that he did not taste death in the usual way. One day while walking with God, God simply "took him" (Gen. 5:24).

Noah

Noah "found favor in the eyes of the Lord" (Gen. 6:8). God chose to fellowship with him because Noah desired righteousness. The Bible says that Noah "walked with God," which communicates relationship and intimacy (Gen. 6:9). He was so connected to God that he received instructions on how to salvage a righteous remnant by building the ark.

Abraham

Abraham was known as "the friend of God" (James 2:23). God called him out of a foreign land and promised to bless him and make him a great nation. As the first "Father of Faith," Abraham is a perfect example of someone who was unsuspecting when God first spoke to him and set him apart in the land of Ur.

Moses

Moses was called by God and and marked for ministry at birth in the land of bondage. Raised by Pharoah's daughter, he lacked nothing in the material realm. But after he saw the bondage of his people and murdered an Egyptian, he fled to the wilderness as a fugitive. God sought him out there and spoke to him through the burning bush. God revealed Himself there as the God of Abraham, Isaac and Jacob—the three patriarchs of the faith who beautifully illustrate God's multigenerational covenant. It was in the desert that God initiated His relationship with Moses, the deliverer.

David

David is described in the Bible as "a man after [God's] own heart" (Acts 13:22). He had a very unique relationship with God. Although he did not always follow the prescribed rules, David was a seeker of God's heart and was ultimately God's choice for the throne of Israel. The reason David held a "special" place in God's heart could very well be because David responded to God's call consistently. Imperfect, impetuous and sometimes irrational, the shepherd boy knew the true Shepherd.

This list of Bible characters reflects God's dogged determination to initiate and relentlessly pursue relationship. Intimate fellowship and relationship have been God's idea, not man's! Down through the annals of time, people have simply made themselves available to Him.

When Jesus came into history's view, He came speaking the same words of His Father, which had been misunderstood for years. God was still speaking words that beckoned the weary to rest, the thirsty to drink and the dead to be born again. Jesus, as God's voice, threatened the religious leaders of the day who thought they had already figured God out. Having systematically removed the relationship factor from the worship of God's holiness and reduced their religious rites to a regimen of rules alone, the religious leaders could not discern the voice of the true Shepherd of Israel.

Read Matthew 5:17–20. Why did the religious leaders of

Jesus' day get upset with Him when He preached?

_____

_____

▲▲▲▲▲▲▲

Read Mark 14:35–36. Jesus constantly referred to God as His Father. How did He address the Father when He was praying in the Garden of Gethsemane just before He was crucified?

_____

_____

▲▲▲▲▲▲▲

When Jesus said "Abba," He was calling His Father "Daddy." The word *Abba* is an endearing term used by little children when they speak to their fathers. Calling God *Daddy* was a radical concept for the Jews, because no one related to the holy God of Israel as a daddy who had tender affection for his little ones. Yet this is how Jesus portrayed His relationship with God Almighty!

PSALM 33:18–22, NIV

This psalm reveals how close our heavenly Father wants to be to those who seek Him. He is not a distant, uncaring God. He longs to be near us!

But the eyes of the LORD are on those who fear him,
    on those whose hope is in his unfailing love,
to deliver them from death
    and keep them alive in famine.

We wait in hope for the LORD;
    he is our help and our shield.
In him our hearts rejoice,
    for we trust in his holy name.
May your unfailing love rest upon us, O LORD,
    even as we put our hope in you.

DISCOVERING TRUE WORSHIP

Since true worship is about relationship, in some ways it is not surprising that the conversation between Jesus and the woman at the well culminates in a discussion about where to worship. The issue is over two mountain peaks in Palestine, Moriah and Gerizim. Jesus points out some hard, cold facts about this woman's questionable lifestyle, to which she comments that He must be a prophet. (This was a brilliant deduction, as He seemed to be reading her mail!) She continues with questions about the Jews' place of worship as compared to the Samaritans'.

Read John 4:20. What did the woman at the well say to Jesus?

_____

_____

▲▲▲▲▲▲▲

How did Jesus respond to her remark in each of the following verses?
John 4:21:

_____

John 4:23:

_____

▲▲▲▲▲▲▲

The Jews worshiped on Mount Moriah, the place where Abraham offered Isaac as a sacrifice to the Lord. It is where David purchased the threshing floor to build an altar and where Solomon ultimately built the temple in the heart of Jerusalem. The Jews were instructed to pilgrimage there three times per year for various important feasts, festivals and sacrifices. *Moriah* means "seen of Yah," or "God sees."

The Samaritans worshiped on Mount Gerizim. Many things could be said about Mount Gerizim and the symbolism it portrays in this story. Located in a particular region of Samaria, it was the place where Moses instructed the people to read the curses for disobeying the law of God. Known as the Mount of Cursing, Gerizim literally means "cut off." It wouldn't seem a very likely place for the worship of God. But it does reinforce one aspect of His character: He is a God of rules and expects undying loyalty. Nevertheless, rules without relationship produce rebellion, as is graphically depicted here.

It must be understood that the Samaritans were a people proud of their heritage and worship traditions. Historically and biblically, their roots as a mixed and crossbred people group can be traced back to earlier than 700 B.C. (Read 2 Kings 17.)

Hoshea was the king of Israel at that time and did evil in the sight of the Lord. Like his fathers before him, he was responsible for allowing and advocating idolatry in the land. The things that the Lord told the Israelites not to do are the very things into which Hoshea led the people. The list included:

- ▲ Worshiping other gods
- ▲ Walking in the customs of other nations
- ▲ Building "high places" of worship to foreign gods, including sacred pillars and Asherim, honoring female deities
- ▲ Speaking against the Lord
- ▲ Rejecting the statutes, the covenant and commandments
- ▲ Creating molten images in the form of calves
- ▲ Worshiping the stars
- ▲ Serving Baal, a foreign god
- ▲ Sacrificing their children in the fire
- ▲ Practicing divination, enchantments and witchcraft

As if that weren't enough, God sent many prophets to warn them of their evil ways. But they refused to listen and obey the Word of the Lord. Instead they "stiffened their necks" because they did not believe the Lord was their true God. Therefore, in His anger, the Lord brought judgment upon the land by raising up the king of Assyria to invade and take them captive.

After leading the Israelites into captivity, the king of Assyria delved into his menagerie of other captive people and selected six different groups from neighboring nations to go back to the land of Israel and resettle in Samaria. They went to Samaria with their wives and children, their

God is a God of rules and expects undying loyalty.

foreign customs, foreign gods and household idols.

In the beginning they did not fear the Lord, so He sent lions among them, which killed some. They cried out in fear to the king of Assyria and said, "We don't know the custom of the god of this land, and so he's sent lions to eat us. Please send someone to teach us." The king did just that—he sent a priest back to Samaria to educate the people in the religion of Jehovah God. As a result, the people worshiped the Lord God and their idols.

Over the course of the next three hundred years, the Samaritans began to hunger after this Jehovah religion. Though it took some time, they started a "clean-up program" and commenced with putting away their idols. But the Jews in Jerusalem would still have nothing to do with these "half-breed" heathens. They continued to believe that the Samaritans were indeed impure in their approach to God, filled with mixture and pride.

Around this same time, Nehemiah began his holy quest of rebuilding the walls of Jerusalem. He was met with some serious opposition and antagonism from Sanballat, the governor of Samaria (Neh. 4:1). After much harassment, in 409 B.C. Alexander the Great finally granted Sanballat permission to build a duplicate temple in Samaria—just like the one in Jerusalem. Consequently, in rebellion, the Samaritans built their temple to worship God, adopted the Pentateuch as their religious book and established rival worship in Samaria. Although they had received the Law, they rejected the prophets—because that was a "Jewish thing."

This historical account became a pivotal point in Jesus' conversation with the woman at the well.

Read John 4:23. Who did Jesus say was seeking worshipers?

_____

▲▲▲▲▲▲▲

Read John 4:24. What did Jesus say to this woman about true worship?

_____

_____

▲▲▲▲▲▲▲

> When Sanballat heard that we were rebuilding the wall, he became furious and very angry and mocked the Jews.
> —Nehemiah 4:1

Jesus blasted the ancient paradigm that the activity of worship must occur in a temple on some specific mountain. Evidently the concept of worship had been reduced to a stated time and place. Prescribed methods and procedures accompanied the worshipers in their approach to *Yahweh*.

Next, Jesus challenged the fundamental validity of the woman's religion by saying she and her predecessors really didn't know whom they were worshiping. His boldness at declaring that salvation would come through the Jewish line could have been interpreted as audacious.

Then He referred to God as Father or *Abba*. This lady had never before heard such seeming casual, familiarity used toward the ancient Yahweh God. Who knows, she may have even thought He was blaspheming. Except for what seemed to be His fortunetelling routine, His behavior could have seemed crazy to her. But with her own sordid history, she wasn't about to be the pot calling the kettle black.

Finally Jesus said that true worshipers would worship *Abba* in spirit and truth. It was worshipers like that for whom the Father was searching! This was a brand-new concept to her. God is searching for worshipers? Not worship? Fundamentally, He was saying that God was looking for and desired the heart more than the offering.

Taken aback for sure, she responded by saying, "I know that Messiah is coming (He who is called Christ); when that One comes, He will declare all things to us" (John 4:25). Interesting thought here—*How did she know that?* The Samaritans did not accept the prophets or their writings about Messiah. She probably heard by way of hearsay that there would be a deliverer some day who would set them free from Roman rule.

What Jesus says next is earthshaking! He literally calls Himself "I AM." Who else would have such authority to say these things but the Son of God? With that statement, He positioned Himself to be equal with God and thus qualified to give voice to God's desire for worshipers.

▲ God was
▲ looking for and
▲ desired the
▲ heart more than
▲ the offering.

GOD IS SEEKING US!

According to the Scriptures, God is seeking worshipers—NOT worship! He's looking for you! As it was in the beginning when He created man, the heart of God still longs for His creation to desire Him as well. He wants to fellowship with us.

Read 2 Chronicles 16:9. What does the Bible say God is looking for?

_____

_____

▲▲▲▲▲▲▲

Read John 6:44. What is necessary in order for a person to come to God?

_____

_____

▲▲▲▲▲▲▲

We sing many worship songs today about searching for God, following hard after Him, worshiping with all our hearts, giving everything to Him, waiting upon Him, finding out what He likes and presenting that to Him. Simply stated, those are the qualities of a radically devoted Christian life—synonyms for true discipleship.

▲▲

God is tenacious in His search for worshipers. We should also be tenacious in our search for Him.

▲▲

But this passionate seeking of God should not be viewed as a performance-based activity. We can't fall into the trap of saying, "If I do all the right things, then God will…" It is true that we must seek God; however, we must realize that if God is searching for worshipers, that must mean He's initiating the drawing. Yes, I search for and seek Him, but He's the One who began the pursuit because He wanted me before I ever knew that I wanted Him. If the Father is seeking worshipers, then there are some things we must understand about His pursuit of us as we pursue Him in return.

Do you remember playing hide-and-seek as a child? When

I was growing up in northern California, on summer evenings we were allowed to stay outside later than normal. We'd play games with the neighborhood kids, games like cowboys and Indians, cops and robbers, sardines, kick the can, blindman's bluff and hide-and-seek. We'd have contests to see who could find the most elusive hiding places, as our goal was to make the seeker work hard at finding us. At dusk on our cul-de-sac it wasn't that difficult finding good places to hide, especially in and around the empty lot next door.

The person who was "IT" would search for the others while we waited patiently for long periods of time in silence. Then we would sneakily make our appearance and run for home base. The trick was to outrun the seeker, and the fun was in creating new hiding places. Of course we would only share the knowledge of those hiding places with our best friend—the only one who knew our secrets.

Now as an adult in my relationship with God, I want to make it easy for Him to find me. Though I sometimes hide from Him because of my sin, I honestly desire to remain open to Him without the games. Consciously, I make every effort to be available to His calling. There's a reciprocation factor in this as well. He searches for me; I search for Him. He pursues me; I pursue Him—and so on.

Sometimes it seems that God is hiding from me. Have you felt that way? The key is in understanding the pursuit. God is tenacious in His search for worshipers. We should also be tenacious in our search for Him. How badly do you want to find Him? He's really only a prayer away—though at times it may seem that He lives on the planet Pluto! The Scriptures clearly teach that if you seek Him with all your heart you will find Him (Jer. 29:13).

> You will seek Me and find Me, when you search for Me with all your heart.
> —Jeremiah 29:13

I AM THINE, O LORD

This classic hymn was written by Fanny Crosby (1820–1915), who wrote more than eight thousand hymns in her lifetime. Blinded in childhood, she grew up in poverty and never even learned to write her name until age eighty. She composed her hymns in her head, and friends wrote them down for her. This hymn, one of her most popular, extols the nearness of God's presence.

I am Thine, O Lord, I have heard Thy voice,
And it told Thy love to me;
But I long to rise in the arms of faith,
And be closer drawn to Thee.

Draw me nearer, nearer, blessed Lord,
To the cross where Thou hast died;
Draw me nearer, nearer, nearer, blessed Lord,
To thy precious, bleeding side.

O the pure delight of a single hour
That before Thy throne I spend;
When I kneel in prayer, and with Thee, my God,
I commune as friend with friend![1]

WORSHIP IS NOT A *RELIGIOUS* THING!

Many people believe *worship* is something religious performed only on Sundays. Others think it is an internal feeling that makes them want to sing or simply an emotional disposition of piety and devotion. But simply being a person who performs a holy-looking or religious duty that is called *worship* is a ridiculous idea in light of the Scriptures. Worship is not just an external act.

Read Amos 5:21–23. In the Old Testament, God often rebuked the Jewish people for doing religious things while their hearts were not seeking God. How did God say He felt about the religious services of His backslidden people?

_____

_____

▲▲▲▲▲▲▲

Read Matthew 15:7–9. Jesus quoted the prophet Isaiah when He rebuked the religious leaders of His day for being religious. What did Jesus tell them?

_____

_____

▲▲▲▲▲▲▲

Read Proverbs 15:8. How does God view the religious "sacrifices" of people who don't seek Him?

_____

_____

▲▲▲▲▲▲▲

Everyone can offer worship, but that doesn't mean that everyone is a worshiper. Many heathens give their time and money to attend a worship service every Sunday for an hour. Then they proceed to restaurants, theaters, sporting events and other entertaining activities, where they invest their lives emotionally and spiritually. For some, *worship* of God in a church building is considered a duty to be done before they indulge in personal pleasures. That may be noble, but silly. Many of these people are ignorantly hiding from God, often behind the façade of good religious duties.

A subconscious but misguided idea about worship is that it is for *conscience cleansing*. The fact that some people go to church, sing the songs, take holy communion, confess their sins and put twenty dollars in the offering before they go home feeling better is NOT worship. Doing "the right thing" on Sunday clears their consciences, but the presence of the Almighty has not been allowed to touch them to the point of causing significant life changes. Unfortunately, many individuals repeat this behavior week after week and never truly worship God.

So here's the million-dollar question. Does God receive morning worship activity on Sunday when lives are focused on their own personal pleasure 95 percent of the time? Is the performance of some form of religious exercise enough to appease the holiness of God and the conscience? Wouldn't that be similar to working eighty hours a week, then doing the dishes on the weekend to prove you love your wife? To whom are you married, to her or your job?

The Father is not interested in worship activities where hearts are not invested. Worship is much more than giving an hour or two per week to the service of the sanctuary. Worship is an all-inclusive lifestyle that reflects God's relational ownership. And that's what He seeks.

Read Psalm 51:15–17. What did the psalmist say God is looking for in our worship?

_____

_____

▲▲▲▲▲▲▲

With regard to Old Testament theology, David's understanding of God's mind and intent in a system that required people to sacrifice animals to obtain forgiveness of sins is revolutionary. God instituted the sacrificial system as a "type" or "shadow" of Christ's ultimate sacrifice that would follow two thousand years later. But David takes the revelation to a whole new level of understanding about worship. David understood that it wasn't the sacrifice itself that God was interested in—it was the heart with which it was offered! True sacrifice, he says, is a "broken spirit; a broken and contrite heart" (Ps. 51:17).

▲▲▲▲▲▲▲▲▲▲▲▲▲▲▲▲▲▲▲▲▲▲▲▲▲▲▲▲▲▲▲▲▲▲▲▲▲▲

Worship is an all-inclusive lifestyle that reflects God's relational ownership.

▲▲▲▲▲▲▲▲▲▲▲▲▲▲▲▲▲▲▲▲▲▲▲▲▲▲▲▲▲▲▲▲▲▲▲▲▲▲

Read 1 Samuel 15:22. How did the prophet Samuel declare this truth to King Saul?

_____

_____

▲▲▲▲▲▲▲

Saul had a rude awakening when he decided to assume the role of a priest in Samuel's absence. Saul was more concerned with what the people would think of him than what God thought of him. That very day God stripped the kingdom from Saul. Samuel made it clear that God delights in obedience to Him more than He does in the actual sacrifice of worship!

The breath or spirit of worship is genuinely depicted through the heart of the one who offers it. It's not worship itself that honors God, but the worshiper. The heart of worship is in the worshiper. And a lifestyle of worship is concentrated devotion to God, to His desires and purposes in every aspect of daily life. It is intensely radical discipleship based on love for God, generated by His relentless pursuit of us. Consequently, it's crucial to understand that His call is not shortsighted—it consumes our entire beings.

The third chapter of Colossians illustrates the sum total of a life presented to the Lord as worship. (Read Colossians 3:17–24.) In verse 17 we read, "And whatever you do in word or deed, do all in the name of the Lord Jesus, giving thanks through Him to God the Father." WOW! What a powerful verse. The entirety of the Christian walk of faith, including family life, social and business, can be supported in this one verse.

> It's not worship itself that honors God, but the worshiper.

The passage continues by saying that:

▲ Wives need to submit to their husbands (v. 18).
▲ Husbands must love their wives (v. 19).
▲ Children must be obedient (v. 20).
▲ Fathers are not to exasperate their children (v. 21).
▲ Slaves are to obey their masters (v. 22).

It doesn't look like anyone escapes an address from the apostle Paul.

In verses 23–24, the earlier verse is reiterated: "Whatever you do, do your work heartily, as for the Lord rather than for men; knowing that from the Lord you will receive the reward of the inheritance. It is the Lord Christ whom you serve."

These verses make it clear that what we do in this life has eternal significance. The apostle is quick to point out God expects us to treat our daily lives as holy unto the Lord: "Always giving thanks to God the Father for everything, in the name of our Lord Jesus Christ" (Eph. 5:20, NIV). Even our work is considered worship to God. No longer is worship a weekend byword. The true worshiper's general view of life can thus be stated: "My life belongs to God, and what I do in life is a reflection of who I am, consecrated and dedicated to God."

Perhaps you're thinking, *Everything I say and do as unto the Lord? That's a totally different perspective of worship than I've ever considered before.* Yes! And I know how difficult it is to maintain a worship perspective when vacuuming the carpet for the twelfth time in a week or delivering those boxes or making those lunches or writing those papers or listening to your coworkers' constant abusive language. But if we limit our worship responses to specific times and places—like Sundays at 10:00 A.M.—we are in danger of shortcircuiting the greater part of our lives from being offered to the Lord.

WORSHIPERS OF YOU

This beautiful chorus celebrates the fact that the Father is seeking devoted worshipers.

Father, You seek
A people that will be
In spirit and in truth
Worshipers of You.
Father, You seek
Hearts that will beat
For You and only You,
Worshipers of You.

Lord, we worship You,
Worship before Your throne.
Lord, we worship You in all the earth.
Lord, we seek You
And we will make You known
'Til all the peoples become Your own,
Worshipers of You.[2]

WORSHIP TWENTY-FOUR HOURS A DAY

In the Twenty-third Psalm, the psalmist said that the Lord prepares "a table before me in the presence of my enemies" (v. 5). This infers that He creates a place of communion and fellowship with Him in any circumstance. He gives us the opportunity to turn our service to others at home, on the job, at school or on the playing field into service to Him.

Sunday's worship time is really no more an act of worship than being a loving parent or spouse, practicing hospitality or doing your job well. It's just a time when we lay aside the necessary but mundane things of life to give full attention and energy to expressing what has become fundamental to our lives.

Are you a true worshiper? In essence, a *worshiper* is one who allows the Holy Spirit to transform his or her life through an act of worship, turning worship into more than just a religious activity. Since worship is more than that, a worshiper knows that the action of worship is merely an avenue for expressing his or her basic disposition toward God.

The worshiper asks these questions often: "Do I perform worship for God, or am I a worshiper? Does my Sunday morning mentality match my Monday afternoon attitude? Am I able to serve others as I would serve Jesus if He were in this situation?" Stated more simply, "Why do I do what I do? Am I endeavoring to please God by this activity, or is this something that is a true overflow of who I am—NOT just what I do?"

Sometimes we get confused about the pursuit of God. We ask questions like, "Why is He after me? What does He really want in return? For Him to accept me, must I perform now at some level of perfection? Are there going to be NEW rules now?" Suddenly, what seemed to be a simple routine of going to church and "paying my dues" turns into some huge monster of a deal.

Relax! It's a matter of trusting your life to the Creator again. Identify your motivation for religious activity that is called *worship*. Determine if your heart is in the activity or if it is just a habit. Does authentic life transpire between you and God at that time? What about any other time?

Remember, God is trying to reach the depths of you. He desires relationship based on mutual love and trust—not fear. Many have a phobic kind of fear of God that keeps them distant from the very light of Life who can make them free. Only God's presence will break down the walls that separate them from the life for which they long.

> ▲ A *worshiper* is one who allows the Holy Spirit to transform his or her life through an act of worship, turning worship into more than just a religious activity.

LET'S TALK ABOUT IT

▲ Jesus introduced a radical concept when He described God as His *Abba* or *Daddy*. How do you think this revelation of God as *Daddy* should affect your relationship with the Lord?

_____

_____

▲▲▲▲▲▲▲

▲ Why is it important for us to recognize that God is the One who initiated our love relationship with Him?

_____

_____

▲▲▲▲▲▲▲

▲ Describe a time in your life when you did outward religious things to please God, yet your heart was not really involved.

_____

_____

▲▲▲▲▲▲▲

▲ Why is it that activities such as church attendance, giving in church offerings, taking communion or helping the poor are not substitutes for true worship?

_____

_____

▲▲▲▲▲▲▲

YOUR TIME WITH GOD

Father, I want to be a passionate worshiper. But I acknowledge that no one can truly worship You unless You draw them to Yourself. So I ask You to draw me. Fill me with passion for You. Thank You for seeking me to be Your worshiper. I don't want just to go through the motions of worship or just to give You lip service. I don't want just to perform religious exercises. I want to give You my heart—fully and completely. Take my heart and make me Your devoted disciple.

CHAPTER THREE

Personal Worship and Private Devotion

S IMON, A PHARISEE, ASKED JESUS TO DINNER ONE EVENING. Perhaps it would be a rather benign meal with some curious seekers. But Jesus knew there was another motive for the invitation. As they reclined at the table, a prostitute from the city came into Simon's house with a beautiful vase filled with costly perfume. (It is said that this exquisite product could have been worth between $5,000–$10,000.)

As she knelt down, she began to weep over Jesus' feet. With her tears she washed them, dried them with her hair, then poured the expensive ointment out over them. After that she kissed His feet and then repeated the entire process.

Well, this was a bit too much for Simon and his other guests. Simon thought to himself, *If Jesus were a prophet, He would know what kind of woman this is.* Jesus knew what Simon was thinking and proceeded to tell a story.

Then Jesus spoke up and answered his thoughts. "Simon," he said to the Pharisee, "I have something to say to you."

"All right, Teacher," Simon replied, "go ahead."

Then Jesus told him this story: "A man loaned money to two people—five hundred pieces of silver to one and fifty pieces to the other. But neither of them could repay him, so he kindly forgave them both, canceling their debts. Who do you suppose loved him more after that?"

Simon answered, "I suppose the one for whom he canceled the larger debt."

"That's right," Jesus said. Then he turned to the woman and said to Simon, "Look at this woman kneeling here. When I entered your home, you didn't offer me water to wash the dust from my feet, but she has washed them with her tears and wiped them with her hair. You didn't give me a kiss of greeting, but she has kissed my feet again and again from the time I first came in.

IN THIS CHAPTER YOU WILL DISCOVER THAT...

▲ Knowing God is a process, just like any relationship.

▲ At some point, each person must come face to face with God's ownership of us.

▲ There are seven important options for deepening your intimacy with God.

You neglected the courtesy of olive oil to anoint my head, but she has anointed my feet with rare perfume."

—LUKE 7:40–46, NLT

There's a powerful picture here worthy of laboring to understand. The guest of honor, Jesus Himself, was reclining at the table and ready to take on the most ruthless of challenges from the group of Pharisees gathered around. Suddenly all eyes turned to the foot of the table. There knelt a woman with a questionable reputation in the community who had come to dinner uninvited.

To make matters worse, she started a dramatic ordeal with her tears, her hair and some incredible perfume that left the room filled with the fragrance. The guests were speechless except for a few gasps.

Our passion for Jesus must be birthed from a personal perspective.

Knowing what His host was thinking, Jesus nailed him to the wall with a poignant story about true love and forgiveness of sins.

The woman in this story clearly illustrated that she was overwhelmed by the mercy of the Savior. His love and forgiveness were what kindled her desire for relationship with Him. She even spent her life savings to purchase an alabaster box of precious ointment, then "wasted" it on the Master's feet. O the depths of pure love poured out as a gift to One so gracious, loving and accepting. He knew everything about her and loved her anyway!

Likewise, our passion for Jesus must be birthed from a personal perspective. The awesome privilege of knowing His saving grace in our lives personally far outweighs the stories we've heard. We can read about the God of the Bible and endeavor to approach Him with intellectual knowledge. We can search the Scriptures, banter about theological ideals and doctrines and impress others with our wisdom. But until we meet Him and realize what He has done for us, we cannot truly know Him nor worship Him. God's heart is for us to know Him and be known by Him.

Read John 5:37–40. In answering His critics, Jesus revealed the reason they did not know God, even though they had searched the Scriptures. What was this reason?

_____

_____

▲▲▲▲▲▲▲

As we read in the previous chapter, Jesus spoke with the woman at the well regarding living water. He was there to provide a new running river in place of the stagnant still water. In that day, rivers were preferable to well water, as the refreshing streams flowing from the mountain heights always brought the best water. God wants us to find our fountain of life in Him daily. The spring of life is fresh every day if we're willing to drink and allow it to satisfy us.

PSALM 15:1–5, NIV

This psalm reminds us that true worship is not about what we do, but _who we are_. It is not just about acts of worship in the congregation, but how we live our lives every day. Worship must be a lifestyle.

Lord, who may dwell in your sanctuary?
    Who may live on your holy hill?

He whose walk is blameless
    and who does what is righteous,
who speaks the truth from his heart
    and has no slander on his tongue,
who does his neighbor no wrong
    and casts no slur on his fellowman,
who despises a vile man
    but honors those who fear the Lord,
who keeps his oath
    even when it hurts,
who lends his money without usury
    and does not accept a bribe against the innocent.

He who does these things
    will never be shaken.

O God, you are my God, earnestly I seek you; my soul thirsts for you, my body longs for you, in a dry and weary land where there is no water. I have seen you in the sanctuary and beheld your power and your glory. Because your love is better than life, my lips will glorify you.

—Psalm 63:1–3, NIV

INTIMACY WITH GOD

The intimacy factor has been a missing ingredient in the church's relationship to God for centuries. There have been those who have longed for and pursued the presence of the Lord through the years (Ps. 63:1–3). Those who do so find their fulfillment in Him. But on a broader scale, the church has been anemic in her understanding and pursuit of intimacy with God. We've heard a lot about it for the last two decades, but we have yet to grasp the intensity of its significance in the lives of individuals and future of the church.

There has been a measure of revelation and understanding that has come to the body of Christ, but I believe the Lord longs to show us something deeper in the area of intimacy in relationship with Him. We must move beyond the obviously superficial outer layer of religious activities alone to the inner realm of knowing His beautiful holiness.

▲▲▲▲▲▲▲▲▲▲▲▲▲▲▲▲▲▲▲▲▲▲▲▲▲▲▲▲▲▲▲▲▲▲▲▲▲▲

Knowing God is a process, just like any relationship.

▲▲▲▲▲▲▲▲▲▲▲▲▲▲▲▲▲▲▲▲▲▲▲▲▲▲▲▲▲▲▲▲▲▲▲▲▲▲

In John 17, Jesus prayed, "And this is eternal life, that they may know You, the only true God, and Jesus Christ whom You have sent" (John 17:3, NKJV). Jesus came to bring life—abundant life. In this verse He declares that eternal life is found in knowing God. Knowing God! How can someone know God?

Knowing God is a process, just like any relationship. The Scriptures tell us that Adam "knew" Eve, and she conceived. The intimacy factor of the knowledge of God makes us one with Him. One of the definitions of the word *to know* in Greek is "an ongoing, progressive revelation." This does not happen through a brief, emotional love encounter. The inference is to an investment of time.

My wife and I have shared almost every kind of experience together in the twenty years we've been married. I can say that I know her pretty well. Now, of course it didn't take that long to get to know her. But my knowledge of her has been progressive through the years. And I learn more about her daily. We often say to each other how we look forward to knowing more about one another after twenty more years.

The length of time we've shared together creates an ease of communication. We don't need to apologize for our feelings any longer. The investment of time and energy we've made into one another gives us the liberty to respond freely about our feelings. Sometimes we surprise each other with our attitudes or comments about things, but that's rare. The intimacy we enjoy is exciting, yet comfortable for the same reasons. But when we slip and begin to take advantage of the other's kindness or grace, we have the freedom to address the issue and pull each other back into line because of the honor we place on our relationship.

This is the kind of intimate friendship and relationship Jesus wants with His bride. You've probably heard it said that He will return for a *bride*, not a weekend *girlfriend*. The difference is the depth of commitment as a result of the time invested. Are we just looking for a "feel good" time, or is there something else of permanent value that we recognize, are willing to invest in and for which we will sacrifice?

Read John 17:20–21. In the Garden of Gethsemane, Jesus prayed that all believers would find intimacy with God and unity with each other. What is one of the results of such intimacy?

_____

_____

▲▲▲▲▲▲▲

Read Ephesians 5:30–32. The apostle Paul described the closeness we can have with God by comparing it to what human relationship?

_____

_____

▲▲▲▲▲▲▲

Read Isaiah 29:13–14. Is it possible to worship God outwardly in religious practice without worshiping Him inwardly?

_____

_____

▲▲▲▲▲▲▲

Luke 10:38–42 tells us the story of Mary and Martha, two sisters who had a close friendship with Jesus. It seems as though Martha was doing all the work in the kitchen while Mary was listening to Jesus' teaching. If we read the story and accept it at face value, it would seem that Jesus was rebuking Martha for being more concerned with hospitality while affirming Mary for being lazy—sitting and listening to Him. But a deeper look into the cultural significance of this scene shows something more revealing about the intensity of personal relationship.

In the custom of the day, students of the Torah would be taught as they sat at the rabbi's feet. They would listen and perform their studies with the oversight of the teacher who shared personal experiences of life skills through the teaching. Women in that day were not privileged to learn. Their job was to keep the house and serve only. Naturally when company would come, Martha and Mary would repair to the housework and kitchen duties while their brother, Lazarus, would join Jesus and others to talk about important matters.

On this particular day, however, Mary decided to stay in the room to listen and learn from the Master—a cultural faux pas for women. Instead of rebuking Mary for such seeming arrogance in role confusion, Jesus affirmed her position as a disciple and said she had chosen the good thing, which would not be taken from her. Mary laid aside her pride, the fear of men, the concern of what others would think of her cultural ineptitude and cast herself at the feet of Jesus. She loved Him and wanted to know Him!

As we've already discussed, God is initiating this passionate, learning relationship. He longs for those who will accept His invitation to love and be loved in the deepest way imaginable.

> Is Jesus Lord ▲
> and Master, or is ▲
> He an additive to ▲
> your weekend life ▲
> as Sweet'n Low ▲
> is to iced tea? ▲

Those who will walk side by side with Him in a manner destined for His favorites. (And everyone has the potential to be His favorite.) His pursuit is relentless, and He patiently waits for our response.

As we discovered in the last chapter, the Father is more interested in who we are on the inside than our outward religious activities. Simply said, what is on the inside is manifested outwardly. Jesus made that clear to the Pharisees when He said, "It's what comes out of the man that defiles him" (Mark 7:21–23, TLB). By watching and listening to Jesus, it doesn't take long to recognize the depth of character that God wants to develop in us through daily relationship building. It is inane to expect that we can access everything we need from God through the Sunday morning worship gathering.

We must accept the fact that cultivating any relationship takes time, which is our most precious commodity. We must ask ourselves the question, "What is this worth?" Because Jesus purchased us for God, we belong to Him. Personal worship and private devotion are based on ownership. So, if indeed ownership is the issue, to whom do you think you belong? In the compartmentalization of your busy life, where is the greatest amount of your affection invested? Is Jesus Lord and Master, or is He an additive to your weekend life as Sweet'n Low is to iced tea?

At some point each person must come face to face with God's ownership of us. It's really the only way we can truly receive His love. If He owns us by way of a legal purchase agreement, then He must have a vested interest in His possession. He wanted us, so He bought us with His blood. And He's in hot pursuit of those who desire to receive His love. I think you would concur that you desire to receive His love— but are you willing to make the necessary adjustments in your life and schedule to position yourself where you can actually *receive* that love, not just talk about how wonderful it is?

GOD'S ROYAL PRIESTHOOD

Referring to the "priesthood" of the believer often brings up a barrage of mental pictures, usually related to our experiences

> For from within, out of men's hearts, come evil thoughts of lust, theft, murder, adultery, wanting what belongs to others, wickedness, deceit, lewdness, envy, slander, pride, and all other folly. All these vile things come from within; they are what pollute you and make you unfit for God.
> —Mark 7:21–23, TLB

with traditional church decorum. We reflect on the vestments, the incense and the formal procedure with its specified criteria. Sometimes the ritual of the ceremony itself camouflages the reality of the relationship God has established in biblical, historical and spiritual protocol. The *form* becomes the obstacle that hinders us from grasping truth about God's ethics, standards and moral perspectives.

Based on the Old Testament pattern, the priesthood adhered to precise regulations. (Read Exodus 28–29.) As a New Covenant royal priesthood, we have similar responsibilities and privileges. The first is to live in the light of His presence. That cannot be considered a weekly visitation option. It must be a cultivated, calculated and inhabited place. The fact that God calls us into His light proves He will equip us to enter.

> But you are a chosen race, a royal priesthood, a holy nation, a people for God's own possession, that you may proclaim the excellencies of Him who has called you out of darkness into His marvelous light.
>
> —1 PETER 2:9, EMPHASIS ADDED

Simply said, God called us out of darkness so that we would proclaim His praises! That is, we are to announce, to demonstrate, to speak out and to declare. The point of this passage is to reinforce God's perspective of eternal fulfillment. He's called us to be priests, those who would stand in the light of His presence to bring sacrifices of worship and to proclaim Him God! This genuinely awesome distinction of honor did not come cheaply—it cost dearly!

Read Hebrews 13:15. What type of sacrifice does God ask us to offer continually to Him?

▲▲▲▲▲▲▲

Read Psalm 22:3. What happens when we offer praise to the Lord?

▲▲▲▲▲▲▲

Through the Old Covenant, God wanted to show us how seriously He takes the worship of His name. He established the priesthood to give us a picture of how we are to respond to Him in the beauty of holiness. The priesthood was not intended to keep people distant! Remember, the Israelites were in bondage for four hundred years and were not allowed to worship their God freely. The new procedure was designed to generate a healthy respect for that which had been lost over the years in Egypt. God set forth the new code of ethics in the Ten Commandments and set up the priesthood as the method of approach to His holiness. It was to be a way of foretelling His plan for the covenant to come.

First, the priests were to identify with the slain sacrifice by laying their hands upon its head. They were then ceremonially washed with water from the laver, which had been constructed from highly polished brass mirrors. Today this is a picture of identifying with Jesus, the sacrificial Lamb, and receiving His shed blood as atonement for sins. Once we accept His atonement, we can view ourselves through the mirror reflection of His Word, cleansed and freed from sin, and given a destiny.

After the ceremonial washing, the priests were anointed with cinnamon, cassia, calamus and olive oil. This preceded the consecration with blood upon their thumbs and toes, which was a picture of being set apart for the service of the Lord in deed. The symbolic imagery here is very specific and extensive as it relates to what Jesus did to fulfill these rites and what He requires of us.

The water of the Word cleanses us to receive the anointing of the Holy Spirit, which sets us apart as His ministers. The consecration is a daily submission of our "walk and talk" to the lordship of Jesus Christ, so that He may be honored in all we say and do. This is a daily apprehension of our calling as a "royal priesthood"—it is not a negotiable alternative. We MUST make a legitimate connection with God daily to be effective in our lives and ministries.

Read Ephesians 5:25–27. What does the "water of the Word" accomplish in our lives?

_____

_____

▲▲▲▲▲▲▲

Read Hebrews 9:11–14. In Bible times, the high priest would offer the blood of animals for the cleansing of people's sins. Who fulfills this role now? What is the result?

_____

_____

▲▲▲▲▲▲▲

Read James 1:22–24. In what way is the Word of God like a mirror?

_____

_____

▲▲▲▲▲▲▲

Read James 1:25. What is the promise given to those who view themselves in light of God's Word?

_____

_____

▲▲▲▲▲▲▲

When the priests were fully cleansed, clothed, anointed and consecrated, they were given some stalks of grain to wave before the Lord as an offering. This was to show that they were ready to worship. Not only were they looking good, smelling good and commissioned for action, but also they were given something to do as a beginning in their ministry.

The Lord cleanses us, purifies us, anoints us and dresses us in robes of righteousness, not just to leave us looking good, but as was previously stated, to commission us for service— that is, "to show forth His praise" and purpose!

There are a number of powerful analogies used in Scripture to illustrate the body of Christ. Through the years God has shown His plans and purposes by revealing to us those truths at strategic times. We are a body, an army, "a chosen race, a royal priesthood, a holy nation" (1 Pet. 2:9). There is an eternal destiny to this pursuit of God.

It's true; God relates to us in many ways. Because our history is already written in Him, He also relates to us as He will in eternity—to us as His bride. He longs to captivate her heart by captivating her value system. What is important to Him must be important to her—becoming so aware of His presence that one glance can communicate a world of emotion and spiritual awakening. "We were created to be driven by passion, ecstatic in the transcendent beauty of God."[1]

There's really no other way than to give of ourselves to Him through daily devotion and private worship. There is a deep work of relationship that is essential in developing an ear that hears the voice of the Bridegroom.

NEAR TO THE HEART OF GOD

This famous hymn by Cleland McAfee calls us to a place of "quiet rest" that can only be found in God's presence. A Presbyterian pastor in Missouri, Cleland wrote the song in 1897 to comfort his family in a time of tragedy. The hymn was first sung outside a darkened, quarantined house where two of his nieces died of diphtheria.

There is a place of quiet rest,
Near to the heart of God,
A place where sin cannot molest,
Near to the heart of God.

O Jesus, blest Redeemer,
Sent from the heart of God,
Hold us who wait before Thee
Near to the heart of God.[2]

DEVELOPING YOUR DEVOTIONAL LIFE

"So, how do I develop a daily devotional life?" you ask. Perhaps it's a *time* issue. There's no way you can pack one more thing into your already overly busy life. But if your devotional life is viewed as an *addendum* to your life and not the *source* of life, defeat is inevitable. Here's a general format of options that may help you set sail on your quest for an intimate awareness of God's presence.

1. Begin with repentance.

You're going to like this—your journey must begin with repentance, including an acknowledgment of the lack of genuine desire for God and a willingness to be changed by His loving embrace. This doesn't have to be monumental; nevertheless, it is imperative to get started. Repentance must become a lifestyle choice and an act of worship. The process of changing our minds and hearts to be like Jesus will take the rest of our lives. Let the repentance commence so we can begin to know Him!

In the process of repentance, it's natural to make a mental checklist of questions considering how to keep our love life with God fresh and vibrant. The list probably begins with something like this: "Is it going to be fruitful this time? I've tried this before, and it was a flop. I really don't want to spend time on something that will not produce quick results. And after so many failed attempts at New Year resolutions, I don't want to begin something else that I won't finish. There's too much wasted money invested in exercise equipment that now sits dormant, begging for someone to use. If this is another *exercise*, I hope it turns out better than my short-lived physical regimen."

There's hope! Though disciplines are often tedious and tasteless, this one has benefits that far outweigh the basic rule of "no pain, no gain"! Experts say it takes the human mind twenty-one days to establish a habit. After that, it's a matter of maintenance. So first determine if you are a morning person or a night person. Some operate more clearly in the morning, others in the evening. Find out when you can give the best moments of your attention to God. Then buckle your seatbelt—you are embarking on the journey of a lifetime with the God of the universe who knows your name and is beckoning you to follow Him. Welcome aboard!

Read Mark 2:16–17. Why is repentance important?

_____

_____

▲▲▲▲▲▲▲

Read Romans 2:4. What is the motivating factor behind God's asking us to repent?

_____

_____

▲▲▲▲▲▲▲

2. Keep it simple.

In the apostle Paul's second letter to the church at Corinth he shares his concern: "But I am afraid, lest as the serpent deceived Eve by his craftiness, your minds should be led astray from the simplicity and purity of devotion to Christ" (2 Cor. 11:3). In contemporary words, *complication hinders communion!* Do not make your pursuit of God complicated. It cannot be filled with a list of rules and regulations that spout out answers for everything. Don't forget, this is a divine relationship we're talking about.

▲ ▲

Buckle your seatbelt—you are embarking on the journey of a lifetime with the God of the universe who knows your name and is beckoning you to follow Him.

▲ ▲

"The simplicity of pure devotion to Christ! The primary element here is 'devotion to Christ,' and we must make that as simple as possible. From the depths of our souls comes a cry to know God simply, truly and deeply without all the trappings and extra baggage that religious endeavors tend to place on us. In our hearts we want to run away from all the formulas that have exhausted us through the years in our attempts to be spiritually acceptable to God."[3] God desires genuine honesty. Jesus said, "Blessed are the pure in heart, for they shall see God" (Matt 5:8). Complete transparency with Him, especially about our weaknesses, is crucial. Openness to Him and His transforming power can only come as we submit to the light of His truth.

3. Find the Lord in the Bible.

It is strategic that the foundation of His personhood and character be studied and experienced through the Scriptures.

All other experiences must stand the test of the authority of His Word.

New believers in Jesus are encouraged to begin their Bible reading in the Gospel of John. It's an easy book to get a clear picture of who Jesus is and how He related to the average person. If you're new to this private devotion thing, I would recommend the same. Find a version of the Bible that makes sense to you and helps you to connect to the truth of Jesus' life, death and resurrection. Read the Scriptures as if the writer were speaking directly to you. (He is!)

▲ Some find it easier to have a devotional guide that segments Bible reading into daily sections for the entire year.

▲ Others prefer reading sections that pertain to their personal life and struggles by topic.

▲ Personal Bible studies are available for studying a theme, a reference, a topic or an entire book.

4. Meditate.

Find a portion of Scripture or a simple devotional nugget of truth and mull it over in your mind. Speak out the truth you grasp from it, and write about it. Commit your thoughts to paper, and allow the Holy Spirit to energize your thinking so that something more than memory work transpires. Then ask the Lord to show you how to apply practically the new-found truth. There's a unique blending of the right brain and left brain with this exercise. The left side of the brain analytically processes thoughts. The right side of the brain creatively expresses the feelings associated with those thoughts so that the soul can be poured out in a systematic way through this kind of meditation.

5. Remember to pray.

Make it a habit to talk to the Lord about everything! "Don't worry about anything; instead, pray about everything. Tell God what you need, and thank him for all he has done" (Phil. 4:6, NLT). Requests are welcome in His presence. "You do not have because you do not ask" (James 4:2). The Lord invites us to take Him at His Word and ask for what we need. Jesus told His disciples, "Your Father knows what you need, before you ask Him" (Matt. 6:8). So—ASK!

6. Listen.

Quiet yourself to the point of internal peace, and allow the Spirit of God to speak to you. Put aside your important daily "to do" list, and focus your attention on hearing His still, small voice inside you. He lives in you and has great secrets to share—listen to Him.

AS THE DEER

Many churches today sing this simple chorus, which focuses on our individual need to drink from the Lord's presence.

As the deer panteth for the water
So my soul longeth after Thee.
You alone are my heart's desire,
And I long to worship Thee.

You alone are my strength, my shield;
To You alone may my spirit yield.
You alone are my heart's desire,
And I long to worship Thee.[4]

---

7. Pursue Him in worship.

Since worship is a heart connection to the person and character of God, designate a time for your heart to communicate with Him. You may ask, "Is singing worship? I don't sing well…" Singing is only a vehicle for worship. True worship is birthed from a grateful heart that needs to be expressed. But do understand—"feeling grateful" is not an expression of worship. Worship must be communicated. The Bible teaches that thanksgiving is in the heart, but blessing comes out of the mouth (Ps. 63:3–5). With words through your mouth, communicate your love for God. Speak, sing, hum, play an instrument! Tell Him how great He is, and thank Him for His mercies, which are new today!

There are many tools available to us today—prayer journals,

Because your love is better than life, my lips will glorify you. I will praise you as long as I live, and in your name I will lift up my hands. My soul will be satisfied as with the richest of foods; with singing lips my mouth will praise you.
—Psalm 63:3–5, NIV

devotional books and specialized Bibles for men, women and children, Scripture memory aids, daily workbooks of all sorts, to name but a few. With all this at our fingertips, it would seem that we could master the art of the pursuit of God. However, the travesty of relationship retardation in the church still remains. If only we could grab hold of this principle—the true knowledge of God and the residual fulfillment in our lives is based on what we're willing to give for it. It's a value judgment.

One of the most important purposes for personal worship and private devotion is for emotional healing. The Lord desires to touch us deeply in our souls to the point of true wholeness. Many have wrestled for years with life-dominating sin that keeps them down, depressed and ineffective in their walks with God. They pray and cry out to God in desperation on occasion, but regularly feel isolated and alone in their fight. If this describes your experience, there is hope for you in your struggle. But it will take some commitment to break through to wholeness. The Lord is calling you to fervency in your personal pursuit of Him. This is the only way to be truly free. He longs to meet you in your area of struggle if you will but make the time and create the opportunity for Him to reveal Himself in your life.

There do seem to be random moments when God "shows up" in our lives, breaking in on an ordinary day to ruin us for the mundane. I love those times when, unannounced, He boldly draws back the curtain of heaven and steps into my boring reality simply to remind me that He is there and in charge of my life!

However, I've missed many of those times because I was not prepared for His appearing. As Jesus relayed in the parable of the ten wise and foolish virgins, half of them weren't prepared for the Bridegroom and were called foolish because their oil had run out. (Read Matthew 25:1–13.) In order to keep our lamps trimmed and burning, we must stay linked to the oil provider.

If the oil is a picture of the Holy Spirit, He must be able to

The river must continue to flow into us in order to flow out through us.

leak out. The overflowing power of the Holy Spirit has to be replenished when it is used up or given out. The river must continue to *flow into us* in order to *flow out through us.* Even Jesus had times of refreshing with the Father after a long day of ministry. He recognized His source of power and strength.

Taking the time is the most crucial encouragement I could pass on to you. You cannot afford to miss Him! He's waiting to meet you in the quiet place to share His secrets with you. Don't wait until Sunday morning to meet with God. There's so much more He needs to say to you privately than He can say in a public setting.

Because Jesus has provided us an opportunity to fulfill all our personal longings for intimacy with Him in the secret place, I say take advantage of that opportunity to know Him deeply and be changed by His overwhelming love. The embrace of God is a priceless experience. Let's press on to *know Him* in private so we can *make Him known* in public.

LET'S TALK ABOUT IT

▲ Why do you think it is difficult for some people to find intimacy with God? What types of things can hinder us from finding this closeness with Him?

_____

_____

▲▲▲▲▲▲▲

▲ What are some ways you could find more time each day to develop your relationship with Jesus?

_____

_____

▲▲▲▲▲▲▲

▲ Throughout the Bible we are reminded of the importance of meditating on God's Word. What are the benefits of making the Word a key focus in our devotional life?

_____

_____

▲▲▲▲▲▲▲

▲ Describe a time when you took time to listen to God. What did He say to you?

_____

_____

▲▲▲▲▲▲▲

YOUR TIME WITH GOD

Father, I want to have a more intimate relationship with You. I want to know You more and become more vulnerable and transparent before You so that Your Holy Spirit has more freedom to work in my life. I repent of anything that I have allowed to hinder my walk with You. Cleanse me by the blood of Jesus. Wash my mind with Your Word, and help me to prioritize making more time with You every day so that I can walk in the fullness of Christ.

CHAPTER FOUR

Praise Is...?

THE RECIPE CALLED FOR FLOUR, EGGS, MILK, SUGAR, SALT, VANILLA, BUTTER AND A LITTLE BAKING POWDER. Jake didn't have any baking powder, and he had only one egg instead of three. It was his wife's birthday, and he thought he'd surprise her with a special breakfast. He wasn't that familiar with kitchen apparatus or the formulas necessary to create food. That was Stacy's job...but he didn't think it would be that difficult to improvise his way through a simple breakfast. Whipping up the batter for some killer crepes, he thought he could fudge a bit on the overall recipe by using more flour and milk. I mean, really! What's the big deal with all those eggs anyway? But when he was done, the crepes did not rise and were not fluffy at all due to the lack of baking powder and eggs. OK for pancakes, but a major fiasco for crepes! Even though Stacy was complimentary, he knew he'd blundered the endeavor. *If only I had been more prepared,* he thought. But guys don't typically think that way in the kitchen.

Perhaps the story is familiar in some way. Whether it is in the kitchen, at the office or in the garage, we usually like to feel more in control of our surroundings by having the proper tools, elements or ingredients to work with. When we don't, the "second best" syndrome takes over, creating the feeling of failure. Poor Jake's crepes were definitely a flop, but not completely inedible. With a little fruit, whipped cream and powdered sugar, some of his concoction was indeed salvageable. Not the best, but salvageable. After all, he did his best, right?!

You've heard of things that were jerry-rigged? Some people throw plans together in their lives, hoping everything turns out OK. They don't usually set out to be haphazard about a particular event or occasion, yet when it

IN THIS CHAPTER YOU WILL DISCOVER THAT...

▲ God developed a prescription for worship through His pattern of worship in the tabernacle.

▲ Giving praise to God is the proclamation of His importance or worth.

▲ Acts of praise and worship are demonstrations of giving something to God.

comes down to the wire, they rely on "luck" or "chance" to pull them through—or they resort to what I call "begging prayer." This is the product of remaining uninformed or misinformed.

But maybe you're the opposite of the abovementioned personality type in that everything must be in order before you're comfortable. You do your homework well before embarking on a journey of creativity to spare yourself the remote possibility of embarrassment. You characterize the phrase, "Perfection is preferred, but excellence will be tolerated."

Obviously these are two extremes of control in our lives that the Lord must deal with. He does NOT want us to be ignorant of His ways, but He certainly does not want us to freak out about doing everything right. Jesus came to set us free from a performance-based trap regarding our spiritual exercises! No longer are we bound to the letter of the Law in order to be accepted by God. Now God in Jesus Christ accepts us. Because the Father accepts us, He accepts us as we are in His Son.

PSALM 100:1–5

This celebratory psalm reminds us that heartfelt thanksgiving is a main ingredient of genuine praise.

Shout joyfully to the LORD, all the earth.
Serve the LORD with gladness;
Come before Him with joyful singing.
Know that the LORD Himself is God;
It is He who has made us, and not we ourselves;
We are His people and the sheep of His pasture.

Enter His gates with thanksgiving,
And His courts with praise.
Give thanks to Him; bless His name.
For the LORD is good;
His lovingkindness is everlasting,
And His faithfulness to all generations.

ENTERING GOD'S PRESENCE

There was a prescribed method of coming into the presence of God that was outlined in the Law given to Moses. The priesthood was required to perform a number of duties before actually offering the sacrifice of worship upon the altar. Even the preparations themselves were diligently pursued and followed by the priests to secure their lives in God's presence. If special attention was not given to detail, the high priest might find himself dead in the holy of holies.

The Scriptures imply that the high priest tied a rope around his waist and had bells sewn into his garment so those outside could hear when he moved around. (Read Exodus 28:33–34.) If the bells stopped tinkling, they knew something was wrong. The other priests knew they were not allowed in that particular room in the tabernacle, so they simply pulled his body out with the rope tied to his waist. The next year a new high priest would try again.

As you can imagine, God's holiness was encountered and relatively understood by the way He interacted once per year with the high priest. The brevity of approaching His presence was seen through the sacrifice ritual, and God made it clear that He valued obedience more than the sacrifice itself. But was God actually trying to scare His people away from Him? Absolutely not! He intended to show His great mercy toward them by allowing them glimpses of His greatness—along with His hatred for sin. He knew they could not deal with His complete nature, so He revealed portions of Himself systematically. His desire was to be all His people needed so they would love and follow Him. No other god had demonstrated such miraculous power, and neither had any other god shown such mercy on his subjects.

Though detailed and involved, the prescription for worship in Moses' tabernacle had distinct significance. From the brazen laver in the outer court to the ark of the covenant and the mercy seat in the holy of holies, each piece of furniture played an important role in the drama of Old Testament worship.

One example of the diligent attention given to detail is

found in the anointing oil. The ingredients were extraordinary, and the fragrance was out of this world. Specific instructions were given to the apothecary artisans for the compounding of the oil with which the priests and the tabernacle furniture were to be anointed. Great care was given to the precise measurement of each spice, and every detail was followed for this very expensive creation. It was to be used exclusively for the work of the Lord and not duplicated for any other ordinary purpose. Likewise, it was to be poured on the heads of the priests, those separated unto the Lord, and not to be put upon strangers. (Read Exodus 30.)

> Never assume anything about God that cannot be proven through His Word.

Read James 5:13–15. Oil is a symbol of the Holy Spirit's presence. What significance is there to the biblical command for elders to pray for believers and to anoint them with oil?

_____

_____

▲▲▲▲▲▲▲

Read Hosea 6:6. Many people in Bible times worshiped false gods, who they believed demanded severe sacrifices. How is the true God different in what He demands?

_____

_____

▲▲▲▲▲▲▲

Read Ephesians 2:4–9. We no longer have to struggle for God's acceptance because of Jesus' sacrifice on the cross. What is the basis of our salvation in Him?

_____

_____

▲▲▲▲▲▲▲

Though the symbolism of the anointing oil is quite descriptive of the anointing of the Holy Spirit's sweet-smelling, fragrant aroma, we can gain a clearer view of how serious the Lord is about the worship of His name!

The prescribed way to approach God shows up throughout Israel's annals of history, especially when they began to stray from God's way and do things their own way. One famous instance is found in the life of King David. Overjoyed at the idea of bringing the ark of God's presence back to Jerusalem, David progressed swiftly through the process of preparing a cart to carry it back. After all, the Philistines and other nations transported their idols on carts. It seemed to be the assumed and en vogue method of the day. (Read 2 Samuel 6.)

But when the ark was on its way to the holy city, it became unstable on the cart, and a man reached out his hand to steady it. God struck him dead on the spot! Such a shock! David was grieved, angry and mortified. Why had God done something so terrible? What had David done wrong? He was bringing God's presence to a resting place with the intent of one day building a temple for Him. Didn't God see that?

Noble, but rash! The ark remained in the house of Obed-Edom for three months while David searched out and studied the Law. Painstakingly he found that the ark of the covenant was to be transported on the shoulders of the priests. That was the ONLY way! And someone died to pay for that uninformed decision.

When David's research was complete, he set things in order for the priests to carry the ark properly, being careful not to abuse or misuse the symbol of God's presence. With everything in place, David removed his outer kingly robe and donned the garment of a priest. Then with great exhilaration he danced before the ark as it was carried into Jerusalem. From that day, he was careful not to speculate about what God liked and how God would feel about the treatment of His presence.

David was a man after God's heart (Acts 13:22). He was filled with the spontaneity of praise—he loved being in the presence of God. Until I studied this story intently, I found it surprising that he would even be interested in "the pre-scribed method." The two ideas seem to contradict one another or come from opposite ends of the spectrum. But I

He raised up David to be their king, concerning whom He also testified and said, "I have found David the son of Jesse, a man after My heart, who will do all My will."

—Acts 13:22

believe God taught David a very valuable lesson— not to take for granted the blessing of the Lord. He learned an important message from heaven: Never assume anything about God that cannot be proven through His Word.

David's story with the ark is a dynamic picture of how the Lord sees the worship of His name. Through the centuries many have either speculated about or limited their expressions of worship to human understanding and reason. But God makes it crystal clear in His Word that He does not want us to be ignorant about such things. Through the Old Covenant, God was trying to show the seriousness of sin and point to the cross of Christ. Ultimately, the shed blood of Jesus became the prescribed method by which we are welcomed into the presence of God. Now there's no other way to the Father but through Him (John 14:6).

When David did bring the ark back, he did not place it in the tabernacle of Moses in Gibeon. He set up a new tent for it in Jerusalem and appointed hundreds of singers and musicians who offered praise to the Lord around the clock. (Read 1 Chronicles 16; 25.) These two tabernacles existed simultaneously—one in Gibeon, the other in Jerusalem. In Gibeon, the priests continued to offer animal sacrifices but without song! In Jerusalem, the only record of sacrifice is in music and song, and there was no separation between the people and the presence of God!

This tabernacle of David is the one about which we've heard so much throughout the years. David used a totally unprecedented approach to God, one no one would have dreamed possible. But this young shepherd boy who loved to worship God and eventually became king showed us that worship is more than simply attitude—it is action! He worshiped not because he admired ritual or ceremonial attachments, but because of a heart relationship. And he knew there were benefits to making the Most High his refuge.

> Jesus said to him, "I am the way, and the truth, and the life; no one comes to the Father, but through Me."
> —John 14:6

Read Colossians 3:16. Our walk with God is not based on our experience alone but on the basis of God's Word. What is one way to make sure you live in obedience to what the Bible teaches?

_____

_____

▲▲▲▲▲▲▲

Read John 1:14–15. The apostle John said that the Word became flesh. To whom was he referring?

_____

_____

▲▲▲▲▲▲▲

Read John 14:6–11. How did Jesus say we could come into relationship with God?

_____

_____

▲▲▲▲▲▲▲

REJOICE, THE LORD IS KING

Charles Wesley (1707–1788), brother of revivalist John Wesley, wrote more than six thousand hymns, including "Hark the Herald Angels Sing" and "O for a Thousand Tongues to Sing." This hymn celebrates the kingship and authority of Christ.

Rejoice, the Lord is King:
Your Lord and King adore!
Rejoice, give thanks and sing,
And triumph evermore:
Lift up your heart, lift up your voice!
Rejoice, again I say, rejoice!

Jesus, the Savior reigns,
The God of truth and love;
When He had purged our stains,
He took His seat above:
Lift up your heart, lift up your voice!
Rejoice, again I say, rejoice![1]

THE POWER OF PRAISE

In the Bible, the command to praise occurs more than 330 times. And the directive to rejoice in the Lord is mentioned 288 times. It would seem apparent that God views praising and giving thanks as high spiritual priorities.

Praise comes from a Latin word meaning "value" or "price." Giving praise to God is the proclamation of His importance or worth. Many terms are used to express this in the Bible, including "glory," "blessing," "thanksgiving" and "hallelujah." A transliteration of *hallelujah* from the Hebrew is "praise to *Jah*" or "praise the Lord."

There are many methods of praise, including:

▲ Offering sacrifices (Read Leviticus 7:13.)
▲ Movement (Read 2 Samuel 6:14.)
▲ Silence and meditation (Read Psalm 77:11–12.)
▲ Testimony (Read Psalm 66:16.)
▲ Prayer (Read Philippians 4:6.)
▲ A holy, godly life (Read 1 Peter 1:3–9.)

Yet biblical praise is virtually always connected to music, both instrumental and vocal. (Read Psalm 150:3–5.) Biblical songs of praise vary. Some are personal, spontaneous eruptions of thanksgiving for some redemptive act of God. (Read Exodus 15:1–18; Judges 5; 1 Samuel 2:1–10; Luke 1:46–55, 67–79.) Others are formal psalms and hymns written for corporate worship in the Old Covenant temple. (Read 2 Chronicles 29:30.) Still others were written for the New Covenant church. (Read Colossians 3:16.)

Although there are more than three hundred commands to praise God, the Scriptures also warn us about the quality of praise. Praise and worship must originate from the heart—it is not to become an outward performance only (Matt. 15:8). Corporate praise is to be displayed decently and in order (1 Cor. 14:40). A lifestyle of praise and worship to God is also stressed. (Read Colossians 3:24; Amos 5:21–24.)

Many of the praise and worship expressions mentioned in the Scriptures were exhibited around David's tabernacle and

These people honor me with their lips, but their hearts are far from me. They worship me in vain; their teachings are but rules taught by men.
—Matthew 15:8

But let all things be done properly and in an orderly manner.
—1 Corinthians 14:40

are still culturally functional for today. Let's look at some of these Hebrew and Greek words and consider them "ingredients" for the posture of worship and service to God.

Towdah

Towdah (to-daw')—from the Hebrew word *yadah;* properly, an extension of the hand, i.e. (by implication) *avowal,* or (usually) *adoration;* specifically, a *choir* of worshipers; confession, (sacrifice of) praise, thanks (-giving, offering).[2]

Towdah is an extension of the hand. An example would be raising the hand to offer testimony under oath to affirm a true statement or a confession. This word is specifically used to imply a *choir* of worshipers lifting their hands. It also means "adoration—a sacrifice of praise or a thanksgiving offering."

Enter His gates with thanksgiving [towdah].

—PSALM 100:4

Shabach

Shabach (shaw-bakh')—a primitive root; properly, to *address* in a loud tone, i.e. (specifically) *loud;* figuratively, to *pacify* (as if by words), commend, glory, keep in, praise, still, triumph.[3]

Shabach is to lift the voice in a way that addresses someone of importance. For instance, in the first few centuries A.D., the people would exclaim the emperor as king by shouting, "Hail Caesar!" and ultimately, "Long live the king!"

Because Your lovingkindness is better than life, my lips shall praise [shabach] *You.*

—PSALM 63:3, NKJV

Yadah

Yadah (yaw-daw')—a primitive root; used only as denominative from the Hebrew word *yad;* literally, to *use* (i.e., hold out) *the hand;* physically, to *throw* (a stone, an arrow) at or away; especially to *revere* or *worship* (with extended hands); intensively, to *bemoan* (by wringing the hands): cast (out), (make) confess (-ion), praise, shoot, (give) thank (-ful, -s, -sgiving).[4]

Yadah is an interesting word with several meanings.

Derived from the Hebrew word *yad*, meaning "hand," and *yada*, "to know," the implication in this praise word is that of holding out one's hands toward an intimate embrace. Lifting the hands in this sense is not an admission of surrender but of deliberate desire for closeness with God in worship.

> *Bring my soul out of prison, that I may praise* [yadah] *Your name.*
>
> —PSALM 142:7, NKJV

Zamar

> *Zamar* (*zaw-mar'*)—a primitive root (perhaps identical with *zamar* through the idea of *striking* with the fingers); properly, to *touch* the strings or parts of a musical instrument, i.e. *play* upon it; to make *music*, accompanied by the voice; hence to *celebrate* in song and music: give praise, sing forth praises, psalms.[5]

Zamar means "to pluck the strings of an instrument to accompany singing."

> *Give thanks to the* LORD *with the lyre; sing praises* [zamar] *to Him with a harp of ten strings.*
>
> —PSALM 33:2

Halal

> *Halal* (*haw-lal'*)—a primitive root; to *be clear* (origin of sound, but usually of color); to *shine;* hence, to *make a show,* to *boast;* and thus to *be* (clamorously) *foolish;* to *rave;* causatively to *celebrate;* also to *stultify:* (make) boast (self), celebrate, commend, (deal, make), fool (-ish, -ly), glory, give [light], be (make, feign self) mad (against), give in marriage, [sing, be worthy of] praise, rage, renowned, shine.[6]

Halal is "to celebrate, to show off and boast about God." It's used in a number of ways to support the sense of radical enjoyment. The clarity of sound idea is more related to sight and color, encompassing all the visual demonstrations of worship to God in the regalia of pageantry.

> *Praise* [halal] *the* LORD*!*
>
> —PSALM 150:1

Barak

Barak (*baw-rak'*)—a primitive root; to *kneel;* by implication to *bless* God (as an act of adoration), and (vice-versa) man (as a benefit); also (by euphemism) to *curse* (God or the king, as treason); blaspheme, bless, congratulate, curse, kneel (down), praise, salute, thank.[7]

Barak is a reverent word connoting humility as the worshiper bows or kneels before God in heartfelt thanks.

I will bless [barak] *the LORD at all times.*

—PSALM 34:1

Shachah

Shachah (*shaw-khaw'*)—a primitive root; to *depress,* i.e. *prostrate* (especially reflexive in homage to royalty or God); bow (self) down, crouch, fall down (flat), humbly beseech, do (make) obeisance, do reverence, make to stoop, worship.[8]

Shachah can be seen in the act of lying prostrate before the Lord in deep worship. When there is indubitable recognition of God's holiness, greatness and kingship, often nothing else can express how high He is and how low we are.

O worship [shachah] *the LORD in the beauty of holiness.*

—PSALM 96:9, KJV

Proskuneo

Proskuneo (*pros-koo-neh'-o*)—from Greek *pros* and probably a derivative of *kuon* (meaning to *kiss,* like a dog *licking* his master's hand); to *fawn* or *crouch to,* i.e. (literally or figuratively) *prostrate* oneself in homage (*do reverence* to, *adore*); worship.[9]

Proskuneo is the most common word for worship in the New Testament. It's a very intimate word that conveys a depth of relationship with one's master. Jesus used this word when speaking about worshiping the Father.

But an hour is coming, and now is, when the true worshipers shall worship [proskuneo] *the Father in spirit and truth; for such people the Father seeks to be His worshipers.*

—JOHN 4:23

Tehillah

Tehillah (teh-hil-law')—from the Hebrew *halal*; laudation; specifically (concretely) a *hymn;* praise.[10]

Tehillah is to sing a song and implies the idea of corporate hymn singing. This is where God makes His habitation.

Yet Thou art holy, O Thou who art enthroned upon the praises [tehillah] of Israel.

—PSALM 22:3

Shiyr

Shiyr (sheer)—or (the original form) *shuwr (shoor)* (1 Sam. 18:6); a primitive root [rather identical with Hebrew (*shuwr*) through the idea of *strolling* minstrelsy]; to *sing;* behold [*by mistake for* Hebrew (*shuwr*)], sing (-er, -ing man, -ing woman).[11]

Shiyr is another word for singing. But this word communicates movement combined with song. This associates the concept of "strolling minstrelsy" with an instrument while singing. The word is used when the Israelites crossed the Red Sea and Miriam began a song and dance with her tambourine. There are several words for *sing* in the Bible, and the English translates them 287 times. But less than half of those are mentioned in the Psalms. It seems apparent that singing is an important facet of releasing the emotions of the soul.

Sing [shiyr] *to the* LORD *a new song, for he has done marvelous things; his right hand and his holy arm have worked salvation for him.*

—PSALM 98:1, NIV

Raqad

Raqad (raw-kad'); a primitive root; properly, to *stamp*, i.e. to *spring* about (wildly or for joy); dance, jump, leap, skip.[12]

Raqad, meaning to spin and whirl about in dance, is used to describe King David's display of emotion before the presence of the Lord. This seems to be an individual expression of dance where other words are used to communicate a choreographed team of dancers.

And it came to pass, as the ark of the covenant of the LORD *came to the city of David, that Michal the daughter of Saul looking out at a window saw king David dancing* [raqad] *and playing: and she despised him in her heart.*

—1 CHRONICLES 15:29, KJV

Ranan

Ranan (raw-nan')—a primitive root; properly, to *creak* (or emit a stridulous sound), i.e. to *shout* (usually for joy)— aloud for joy, cry out, be joyful, (greatly, make to) rejoice, (cause to) shout (for joy), (cause to) sing (aloud, for joy, out), triumph.[13]

Ranan is to make piercing noises like shouting or shrieking for joy. Also, singing out aggressively is communicated in this word.

But let all those that put their trust in thee rejoice: let them ever shout [ranan] *for joy, because thou defendest them: let them also that love thy name be joyful in thee.*

—PSALM 5:11, KJV

As we see in these physical expressions, acts of praise and worship are demonstrations of giving something to God! What we have and what we are belong to Jesus, because He, being the essence of all things, purchased us for God. In his letter to the Romans, Paul makes it clear that not only are gratefulness and thanksgiving to be expressed as worship to God, but our bodies are to be presented as living sacrifices to God. He says it is our "spiritual service of worship" (Rom. 12:1). It's not just *words* that God wants—*He wants all of us!* Similar to the commandment of the tithe in the Old Testament, in the New Testament, God wants it all! This is a lifestyle of worship.

> ▲ It's not just
> ▲ *words* that
> ▲ God wants—
> ▲ *He wants all*
> ▲ *of us!*

CLAP YOUR HANDS

This chorus by Bob Kauflin calls God's people to engage in demonstrative praise— with clapping, shouting and the blasts of instruments. Our praise should reflect the majesty of God, and we should not be inhibited when we honor His greatness.

> Clap your hands, all ye nations
> Shout to God with a joyful cry;
> The Lord is King over all the earth,
> How great and awesome is the Lord Most High.
>
> God has ascended amidst shouts of joy
> To the sound of the trumpet and the horn;
> Give Him the glory that is due Him,
> As you sing with all your heart,
> As you sing with all your heart,
> As you sing with all your heart unto the Lord.[14]

AN ACCEPTABLE OFFERING

Psalm 96:8 tells us to "bring an offering, and come into His courts." As we've seen from previously mentioned scriptures, God requires an offering when coming into His presence. Coming empty-handed is not acceptable. Neither God's nature nor His principles have changed simply because Jesus came to earth to see how it really is down here.

In ancient cultures, the practice of gift giving was essential if someone desired to come into the presence of royalty. Even today in many countries this practice is observed. Proverbs 18:16 says, "A man's gift makes room for him, and brings him before great men." The offering creates an open door for an audience with a dignitary or ruler.

The first place we read about the principle of sacrifice is found in the story of Cain and Abel. Abel offered an animal sacrifice to God because he knew that's what God required. Cain, on the other hand, offered the produce of his field, thinking that would pass the scrutiny of God's all-seeing eye. But as the story goes, Cain's offering was not accepted because God required blood to cover sin—not vegetables. Cain was so angry about the rejection of his offering that he killed his brother. Bad attitude, wouldn't you say?

The story of Abraham and Isaac shows us the first mention of sacrifice in worship. God woke Abraham up one morning. "Then God said, 'Take your son, your only son, Isaac, whom you love, and go to the region of Moriah. Sacrifice him there as a burnt offering on one of the mountains I will tell you about'" (Gen. 22:2, NIV).

Imagine what Abraham may have been thinking along the journey up the mountain. Isaac was the son whom God had promised him. Surely he was not delighted at the concept of killing his son. But Abraham had enough faith to believe that if God required this of him, God was faithful enough to resurrect Isaac. Isaac even asked about the sacrifice when he saw there was wood and fire but no animal. Abraham told him that the Lord would provide. So Abraham did what the Lord said—he bound Isaac to the altar and lifted the knife in his hand to slay his son. But then the angel of the Lord appeared to Abraham and said, "Wait! Look, a ram is stuck in the bushes."

Relieved and obviously grateful beyond comprehension, Abraham built an altar to the Lord, naming it "Jehovah Jireh—The Lord Will Provide." A transliteral interpretation would be, "In the mountain of the Lord, He will see to it." Abraham blessed the Lord by acknowledging that what God had required, He provided. God provided Himself a sacrifice.

This is an incredible picture of God providing His Son as the ultimate sacrifice for sin. And through Him we continually offer the sacrifice of praise (Heb. 13:15). In other words, the act of giving sacrifices of praise and worship to the Lord is done through Jesus and His sacrifice. He provides for us what is required in the sacrifice of praise and worship. Even when we don't "feel" like giving thanks, God has already provided that offering if we're willing to accept it and then give it.

Since Jesus came and fulfilled the Law, we no longer need to offer animal sacrifices. As we've already seen in Hebrews 13:15, the New Covenant sacrifice God accepts is the sacrifice of praise. That is the fruit of our lips as they give thanks to His name. Praise upon our lips is an earmark of the Christian walk.

Read 1 John 3:11–12. Why was Cain's offering not acceptable to God?

_____

_____

▲▲▲▲▲▲▲

> Through Him then, let us continually offer up a sacrifice of praise to God, that is, the fruit of lips that give thanks to His name.
>
> —Hebrews 13:15

Read Genesis 22:15–18. What blessing was Abraham promised because of his obedience in being willing to offer God anything He asked?

_____

_____

▲▲▲▲▲▲▲

Read Colossians 1:13–14. What blessing are we promised because of Christ's offering on the cross?

_____

_____

▲▲▲▲▲▲▲

A GRATEFUL HEART

A grateful heart is one of the characteristics of kingdom living. Unfortunately, giving thanks is one of the greatest deficits in the body of Christ. The little (or much) that we may have seems never to be enough to fill us with contentment. Because many have compared themselves to others for so long, the standard of happiness from God's Word has been replaced with feelings of success based on importance, robbing the heart of genuine thanks.

In the first chapter of Romans, we find that God judged certain individuals because they did not acknowledge the God of heaven, nor were they grateful (Rom. 1:21). For these Romans, as it was in the days of Moses when he led the people of Israel out of Egyptian bondage, murmuring was easy! God was indeed angry with them because they continued to gripe about their surroundings and "lack" while choosing to remain distant from Him.

▲▲
A definite way to experience the blessing of God is to give thanks in all things.
▲▲

Complaining about ordinary (or extraordinary) problems in life is natural, especially when it upsets our ideal of comfort. Being uncomfortable causes us to insist on our own way, inferring that God doesn't know what is best for us. Certainly

> For even though they knew God, they did not honor Him as God, or give thanks.
> —Romans 1:21

we must pray about such things and give the reins of our lives into His hands, but we also must assume a posture of gratefulness in the process, even when we don't understand His ways.

As the Lord spoke to the prophet Isaiah centuries ago, "'For my thoughts are not your thoughts, neither are your ways my ways,' declares the LORD" (Isa. 55:8, NIV). The way God thinks is way beyond our ability to grasp. Be that as it may, if we apply our hearts to wisdom and seek His face, the Holy Spirit will reveal the heart of God, for the Spirit searches the hearts and knows the deep things of God (1 Cor. 2:10).

A definite way to experience the blessing of God is to give thanks in all things. (Read 1 Thessalonians 5:18.) In this passage, Paul did not say, "FOR everything you must feel grateful"... that would be ridiculous and humanly impossible. But IN every situation it is possible to choose an attitude of thanksgiving. It is possible to rejoice in suffering for the sake of God's kingdom... counting it all joy when we encounter various trials of faith. (Read James 1:2.)

Read James 1:2–4. What are the benefits to having a grateful heart?

_____

_____

▲▲▲▲▲▲▲

Read Philippians 4:6–7. An attitude of thanksgiving is a key ingredient in receiving what from God?

_____

_____

▲▲▲▲▲▲▲

Read Colossians 4:2. What did the apostle Paul say we needed to add to our prayers?

_____

_____

▲▲▲▲▲▲▲

In the Old Testament Hebrew language, to *give thanks* (*hodah*) was to acknowledge by confession that *Yahweh* was God and King. In a culture filled with the worship of idols

> For to us God revealed them through the Spirit; for the Spirit searches all things, even the depths of God.
> —1 Corinthians 2:10

and false gods, worshipers would *hodah* their gods in recognition of their supposed deity. But God wanted to make it crystal clear that there were to be no other gods!

One of the attributes of God is His holiness. Because God is holy and "wholly other," He is not narcissistic like other gods who focus on themselves. That is one thing that separates Him from others. His heart has always been to bless, nurture and care for His followers. So the command to give thanks shows up as an Old Testament acclamation. Giving thanks to the only true and living God acknowledged the fact that there was no one else to compare. Jesus came to serve. That's what holiness looks like!

In the midst of life's most difficult situations, giving thanks is neither a denial mechanism nor an intended escape from reality. We give thanks because everything is *not* OK, and God is the only One who can give us an eternal perspective. We must see things from His point of view, changing our philosophy of life to fit the faith we confess. In every situation we can acknowledge God as King regardless of whether or not we understand our present circumstances. His love compels us to "come up higher" and see as He sees.

If indeed we are now seated with Christ in heavenly places (Eph. 2:6), His plan is for us to look down upon our enemies and no longer live under the circumstances. This position is secured through the act of giving thanks to God through Christ Jesus. When we seek the Lord, the asking is combined with gratefulness. "Be anxious for nothing, but in everything by prayer and supplication with thanksgiving let your requests be made known to God" (Phil. 4:6).

A heart of prayer with thanksgiving proves humility. The one who is humble enough to ask for help is the one God will help. As it reads in James 4:6, "But He gives a greater grace. Therefore it says, 'God is opposed to the proud, but gives grace to the humble.'"

So, let us view worship as God does. To express sentiments of worship in any of the abovementioned forms is to acknowledge a Power and Presence greater than ourselves who is worth the investment of our lives. Remember—worship is

> And God raised us up with Christ and seated us with him in the heavenly realms in Christ Jesus.
> —Ephesians 2:6, NIV

giving to God. When we recognize what God is worth and give to Him in proportion to His worth, then we are truly worshiping. We know that He's worthy of all praise. But is He worthy of our time, monetary means or the investment of energy for the sake of His kingdom? Worship is placing value on something. It is a treasuring attitude that is expressed in action. He is that valuable!

Worship occurs when, after discovering that our affections have been placed on idolatrous things, we make a correction in order to find our satisfaction in God once again. I worship when I find that I have been trusting in my own abilities and understanding, and I willingly transfer my trust back to the goodness and sovereignty of God.

Jonathan Edwards once said that *religion* consists of our *affections*. Affections arise from the core part of our being and orient our mind, will and emotions toward an object. Our mind, will and emotions are organically connected. It is sin that causes our affections to stray to control, power, comfort and approval. It's amazing how we fantasize and obsess about these things—even speculating how our lives will turn out if we give enough heed to their influence.

Simply stated, control, power, comfort and approval are contemporary forms of idols in our culture that demand attention and obeisance. If we do not repent from following after the falseness of their enticing pleadings, they will consume us!

A devastating trap of idolatry is found in the worship of graven images. "Graven images?" you ask. "This is the twenty-first century. People in the Western world are not archaic enough to worship such things, are they?" But idols do exist today. Unfortunately, as one example, the cancer of Internet pornography is spreading like an epidemic across the world. The eye gate is being consistently defiled through such viewing, creating habitual mental images that thrust many into a life of bondage to idols! And with the reasonable accessibility today, the danger is greater now than ever for men, women and our children. Sadly, the church is no exception.

Repentance is another form of worship. When we renounce our involvement with vain things and repent for violating God's first commandment, there's hope for change. Sin does not have to dominate us. Repentance causes our spiritual senses to be righted and connects us once again to the life-giving source, who is ready to receive our hearts again. Worship then takes on another element, that of lifestyle commitment, as God restores the natural worship instinct in each of us.

Though we've been viewing concepts of worship, worship is more than conceptual. Worship is learning a truth about God and letting it affect you at the core of your being, thus producing a character correction. When we see something profound about God and respond to the revelation by changing our opinion about Him, we have the opportunity to add it to our list of "cool things I learned about God"—or we can allow worship to occur. I prefer the latter.

We have the option of standing outside the holy place to observe God speaking to others, or we can step into life within the holy of holies, inquire of the Lord personally and behold His beauty. His invitation is open, and His commandment is clear.

Come to Me, all who are weary and heavy-laden, and I will give you rest. Take My yoke upon you, and learn from Me, for I am gentle and humble in heart; and you shall find rest for your souls. For My yoke is easy, and My load is light.
—Matthew 11:28–30

LET'S TALK ABOUT IT

▲ Why do you think it is important to understand how to come into the presence of God?

_____

_____

▲▲▲▲▲▲▲

▲ Describe a time where you knew that praising God in a particular situation you were facing made a difference.

_____

_____

▲▲▲▲▲▲▲

▲ This chapter explained the meaning of twelve different Hebrew and Greek words for praise. Describe one definition that was particularly significant to you, and why.

_____

_____

▲▲▲▲▲▲▲

▲ The Bible tells us to be thankful in all things. Why do you think it is difficult for us to do this?

_____

_____

▲▲▲▲▲▲▲

YOUR TIME WITH GOD

Father, thank You for accepting me on the basis of the shed blood of Jesus. I would fall short if I had to approach You on the basis of my own human frailty. Anoint me with the oil of the Holy Spirit. Help me to understand the power of praising You every day, in every situation. Give me a thankful heart that will impact not only my circumstances, but also everything and everyone around me. Teach me to walk in a lifestyle of worship. Amen.

CHAPTER FIVE

The Dynamics of Corporate Worship

IN THIS CHAPTER YOU WILL DISCOVER THAT...

▲ God desires to work in us deeply in private so He can flow through us powerfully in the corporate.

▲ Worship times are intended to connect us with God, to celebrate the resurrection of Jesus and to realize the purpose for our presence in the earth as His hands and feet.

SHE CAME INTO THE SERVICE WITH GREAT EXPECTATIONS OF MEETING WITH GOD INTIMATELY. The week had been extremely difficult, and her need for connection with God was intense. Nancy had recently lost her job, the rent was due and her boyfriend had just informed her that he was interested in someone else. The personal pain she was going through, rivaled only by the abandonment a child feels when left alone on a doorstep, was excruciating. I could only imagine the depths of despair she felt as she came into the worship gathering. Seeing her from a distance that morning, I knew there must be some deep inner conflict in her soul.

Obviously she was thoroughly distracted by her personal need, and God definitely cared about that. His love embraced her, healing her as she wept before His presence that morning. Yet, that day God desired the entire community of believers to worship Him corporately that day. He wanted every believer to connect with Him regarding their pain—not just Nancy.

God wants each believer to connect with Him so that He can heal us. Why heal us? Just to make us feel better so we love Him more? No! It is so we can be more equipped to follow Him and to fulfill His plan for our lives on the earth. It's really not about us—it's about Him!

Fear, shame and emotional pain are facts of life. There's no promise of a stress-free existence. I've heard the saying, "Faith is not the absence of fear; it's our response to it." Simply because I am a believer does not mean I am excused from the trauma of life's difficulties. My response to the problems I face can be either to "run to God" or to "run away from God." Prayer is a true sign of humility. I need the Lord, so I pray—but not only on Sunday morning.

The lifestyle of a worshiper acknowledges God consistently and enjoys communication with Him daily. In the midst of life's most complex and challenging ordeals, the worshiper chooses to believe that God's Word is true.

> The righteous cry and the LORD hears, and delivers them out of all their troubles. The LORD is near to the brokenhearted, and saves those who are crushed in spirit. Many are the afflictions of the righteous; but the LORD delivers him out of them all.
> —PSALM 34:17–19

A recent survey conducted by the Barna Research Group (www.barna.org) revealed that over 90 percent of surveyed adults said worship is very important, but that many struggle to have a consistently positive worship experience. One-third said they always sense the presence of God; one-third said sometimes; and the last third said seldom.

The survey also showed that most people do not personally prepare for worship before the event and struggle to clear their minds to focus on God in worship.

> Without giving themselves time to clear their minds and hearts of their daily distractions and other problems, many people attend a worship event but never enter a worshipful frame of mind. A large share of churchgoers do not pray, meditate, confess or focus on God prior to the start of a church worship event. One consequence is that they find it difficult to connect with Him spiritually. Having never been taught much on worship, they find the inability to interact with God on a deeper level frustrating, but don't know what to do about it.[1]

Though we've already looked at the importance of understanding concepts of praise and worship, and the implication of the personal aspects of the same in private, there are essentially two philosophies of corporate worship.

1. *Corporate worship is designed for God.* He is preeminent. His worth is the focus of the gathering, and what He desires is at the center of attention. Personal fulfillment is achieved through giving God what He deserves and knowing His purpose has been served

and accomplished. The motto is: "God has a plan and exists to receive glory."

2. *Corporate worship is designed for God to meet with individuals.* Personal needs, desires and one's individual feelings about life and God are at the center of attention. Personal fulfillment is achieved by how deep the individual is touched by God. The motto is: "God has a plan, and that is to meet my needs."

One can spend ten minutes in any local church and determine the worship philosophy, which is based on the overall ministry philosophy of that church. Neither the worship philosophy or the ministry philosophy is necessarily more accurate than the other. Yet the pursuit and experience of one philosophy usually takes precedence over the other in a given congregational setting.

Regardless of the "flavor" of worship experience you prefer, or your personality type and past experience, God continues to search for worshipers. He is looking for those whose hearts are fully His. The seasons of life often dictate our ability to receive from God and our ability to respond to God. But we must be aware that to remain in any given "rut" is to shut out the Holy Spirit's maturing power. We may have received a supernatural impartation of revelation at some particular point on our journey, yet it is crucial that we continue to follow the Lord's progression through life and not camp out in any comfortable region.

▲ ▲

Although God's character does not change, His methods often do.

▲ ▲

The Israelites reflected this concept and were notorious for believing things about God that, based on previous understanding, were stale. The manna is a perfect example of holding on to yesterday's truth for today's experience. Although God's character does not change, His methods often do. This confuses many people who hold on to traditions or rituals, thinking that in them there is life. Within the framework of our varied perspectives there is always room for growth and change.

Read Exodus 16:4. How often were the Israelites supposed to gather the "bread from heaven" called manna?

_____

▲▲▲▲▲▲▲

How do you think this correlates with our response to the Word of God today?

_____

_____

▲▲▲▲▲▲▲

Read Isaiah 43:18–19. Sometimes we find change difficult, and we put God in a box and assume His methods are always the same. But what did the Lord reveal to the prophet Isaiah?

_____

_____

▲▲▲▲▲▲▲

Through the natural process of human development, pediatric psychology tells us that one of the first things children are aware of is self. The needs of the body are paramount—food, rest, shelter and affirmation. Though the carnal man is most aware of himself, the spirit of man is most aware of God—the creator of self. As we grow in the Lord, we become more aware of our role as needy children. Through the maturing process we see that we cannot remain in that totally helpless state. We must grow up into the full stature of Christ as a mature man or woman.

Jesus made it clear that the children were welcome in His presence. He even encouraged faith like a child and childlike hearts to trust Him. The challenge for us is to differentiate between "child*like*" and "child*ish*." When it comes to getting our needs met by God, we often demand our own way and use the corporate time of worship to insist on fulfillment. Many have viewed "church" as a time to receive warm feelings from God after a difficult week of fighting the devil… or our boss… Though the warm feelings are available, we often neglect the other side of the picture. God has a purpose for our gathering to worship, and it's not always just to feel good! God's heart is to meet our needs in the presence of the congregation, but this cannot be a substitute for our daily walk with Him.

Our personal relationship with God is in process, as is our corporate relationship with Him. God delights in conforming us to the image of His Son, regardless of the amount of time it may take. As difficult as it is sometimes, everyone must grow.

Growing is the organic effect of natural life, yet it's easy to become content with what is familiar and predictable. For many, the unwillingness to allow spiritual growth to take place is what makes their religious experiences either boring or dead! The life they're looking for is found in the progressive unveiling of God's growth process.

> **God delights in conforming us to the image of His Son.**

When we find personal contentment, love and affirmation with the Lover of our souls in the secret place of private devotion, our needs are less likely to surface and become superimposed on others to fulfill during times of corporate worship. Crying out for God to meet our daily needs is appropriate in private. It is in our private times with our Father that we find our need for emotional fulfillment is met and we sense God's acceptance of us. Crying out to know Him and to be touched by Him is a genuinely intimate request He longs to answer. He desires to work in us deeply in private so He can flow through us powerfully in the corporate.

Read Psalm 34:17. What promise are we given if we cry out to the Lord in times of need?

_____

_____

▲▲▲▲▲▲▲

Read 1 Peter 2:1–3. What is one of the most important things you can do to facilitate spiritual growth in your life?

_____

_____

▲▲▲▲▲▲▲

Read Romans 8:28–30. What happens as we allow ourselves to be conformed to the image of Christ?

_____

_____

▲▲▲▲▲▲▲

Seeking Him earnestly for renewal, revival and the fulfillment of vision is very appropriate for corporate worship. The Lord is waiting for a people who will pray His will and desperately desire what He prioritizes on the earth. He promises to give His blessings to those who hunger and thirst for righteousness (Matt. 5:6). And if we seek His will and kingdom first, then what we need will be granted to us (Matt. 6:33).

So, what are God's priorities for worship in public gatherings? When we meet together for corporate worship we literally become the body of Christ to facilitate the working of His Holy Spirit. I am not the body by myself, nor are you. We are members of the body, and each one has a part to play. As Paul so articulately said, "Just as each of us has one body with many members, and these members do not all have the same function, so in Christ we who are many form one body, and each member belongs to all the others" (Rom. 12:4–5, NIV).

Read Ephesians 5:15–17. Why is it important that we pray according to the will of God?

_____

_____

▲▲▲▲▲▲▲

Read John 6:35. God's blessings are given to those who hunger and thirst for righteousness. What did Jesus say about our hunger being filled?

_____

_____

▲▲▲▲▲▲▲

As a local body of believers, we have responsibilities and obligations to one another through love. God has designed

Blessed are those who hunger and thirst for righteousness, for they shall be satisfied.
—Matthew 5:6

But seek first His kingdom and His righteousness; and all these things shall be added to you.
—Matthew 6:33

specific things for His people to accomplish when they meet together. You've heard the popular phrase, "What would Jesus do?" That's the point of being His body. How would Jesus respond in this situation? There are a number of things He intends for us to achieve while we're together. If we remember that the gathering is for God, set apart for His purpose, we'll see that ministering to Him is our main concern. Worship is for God—we need not be upset if it doesn't meet our criterion for personal gratification.

Christ yearns to shower love upon His bride and to communicate deep things with her in the inner chambers of His courts. His heart longs for shared intimacy resulting from the true knowledge of His intentions. Yet the concept of "bride" is simply the beginning of a long-term relationship where mutual love, understanding, purpose and communication dynamics are established and implemented. There's more to the husband-and-wife relationship than simply romance, albeit thoroughly pleasing to the senses. As the bride of Christ, we have a role to assume that is light-years beyond the sphere of emotional feelings and senses limited by our human bodies and minds.

I'm sure you've encountered times in worship that were "less than" what you felt you needed for that moment. Many have felt that if the worship experience does not touch them in a deeply personal way, then God has not been encountered, nor is He pleased. Therefore, the individual's connection to the experience itself is what receives the most attention—and not God. Hmm…! What does God think? I believe the Lord is more concerned that our hearts and attitudes reflect our desire to express His purpose in our worship experiences with Him than that we pacify our personal moods during worship.

PSALM 133:1-3

This short psalm tells us how God takes special delight in our corporate worship. It is obvious from this passage that our harmony with each other makes our worship attractive to Him.

Behold, how good and how pleasant it is
For brothers to dwell together in unity!
It is like the precious oil upon the head,
Coming down upon the beard,
Even Aaron's beard,
Coming down upon the edge of his robes.
It is like the dew of Hermon,
Coming down upon the mountains of Zion;
For there the Lord commanded the blessing—life forever.

WHY WORSHIP TOGETHER?

Worship times are intended to connect us with God, to celebrate the resurrection of Jesus and to realize the purpose for our presence in the earth as His hands and feet. Let's look at some of those purposes and goals for corporate worship.

1. To minister to the Lord

What does it mean to *minister to the Lord?* To minister to someone is "to attend, care for, wait on, nurture and serve them." Times of worship should be designed to perform service for the Lord. An illustration of this would be a server waiting on a table at an exclusive restaurant.

After being seated, one expects to be asked a number of questions. The query usually begins with, "What is your beverage preference?" Following a list of exquisite specials not printed on the menu, the server allows the patron a season for perusing listed items before a selection is made. At just the right time, the server returns to the table to receive the order and is delighted to make any change necessary to accommodate the specific tastes of the patron.

Timing must be impeccable to suit those being served. Between the first and second course is a brief respite for initial digestion. Then drinks are refreshed. When the main course comes, the patron is observed to see if everything is to his liking. Any necessary adjustments require immediate attention. Of course, during the meal drinks will be freshened again before clearing the dishes for dessert and coffee.

Now obviously, this is a dramatic interpretation of attending a table. But the server here parallels the attitude of the believer. When we minister to the Lord, we are like the server hovering over the table. We ask what would please Him the most, what flavor does He desire or how can we refresh His spirit? "How can we serve You, Master?" is our only concern.

This is also like a personal assistant to a professional in an office, a doctor's clinic, a mechanic's shop or an apprentice to a builder. Whatever the boss wants, he gets. In the meantime, the trainee is being educated. This is not communicating an impersonal treatment of the subordinate. Rather it is as an exercise for ultimate increased authority.

In his book *Improving Your Serve,* Chuck Swindoll talks about those who desire to be great in the kingdom, declaring that they must first learn to be servants.[2] Servanthood is the trademark of those who believe in Jesus, and serving Him is our first priority. Discover what God likes, then see to it that He receives it! Serving Him and ministering to Him ought to be our delight and pleasure. We offer Him our worship as a means of serving Him. As we bless and praise His name, laying aside our personal agendas to focus on His goal, it's fulfilling to know He considers that a place of maturity. In response, it is His delight to meet us at the point of our need.

Celebrating and seeking the Lord is our primary goal. The psalmist said, "One thing I ask of the LORD, this is what I seek: that I may dwell in the house of the LORD all the days of my life, to gaze upon the beauty of the LORD and to seek him in his temple" (Ps. 27:4, NIV).

Read Colossians 3:23–24. Worship includes serving the Lord. What is one of the most practical ways we can serve Him?

_____

_____

▲▲▲▲▲▲▲

Read Matthew 20:27–28. How did Jesus set this example of service for us?

_____

_____

▲▲▲▲▲▲▲

2. To experience the authentic presence of God

We read about Solomon's dedication of the temple and see that the glory of the Lord descended and filled the house. The priests could not even stand up to minister. They experienced God's presence in a way that few have since. What was God's intention when He filled the house with the cloud of His presence? The cloud—a sign of His power and His presence—demonstrated that He desired to dwell with man in a close and tangible way. It was a sign of His favor.

God wants to dwell with us. He wants to abide in the praises of His people, not in houses made by hands. Some have asked why we seldom experience the glory cloud as in days of old. The cloud is representative of the Holy Spirit invading the New Covenant temple, the church. If God's heart is to indwell His people, why would He need to prove He lives in a physical building? Even though He chooses to manifest His presence in unique phenomena on occasion, if we could but grasp the simplicity of pure devotion to Christ, we would see that His goal to bring heaven to earth flows into us and through us by the Spirit whom we cannot see!

Connecting with God is not a mystical or magical thing. It's not about using all the right words like an incantation, or thinking the right thoughts like psychokinesis. It's not about pretending or fantasizing. It's about faith! The writer to the Hebrews said, "And without faith it is impossible to please God, because anyone who comes to him must believe that he exists and that he rewards those who earnestly seek him" (Heb. 11:6, NIV).

God requires faith when we come to Him. We must first believe that He is there and that He desires to meet with us. Regardless of what we may have faced throughout the week, God wants to meet with us as a whole body of believers. He wants to communicate with us His acceptance, His will and His desires so we can be encouraged in our walk of faith and our fight against darkness.

> God wants to communicate with us His acceptance, His will and His desires so we can be encouraged in our walk of faith and our fight against darkness.

Read Isaiah 57:15. God wants people to dwell in His presence, but not everyone chooses to enter in. What characterizes those who enjoy being with Him?

_____

_____

▲▲▲▲▲▲▲

Read Ephesians 6:16. Why is it important to walk in faith?

_____

_____

▲▲▲▲▲▲▲

Based on what many of us have been taught about worship over the years, we think it's holy to concentrate our mental and emotional energy on being *alone* with God in congregational worship. We want no distractions as we personally commune with Him, so we close our eyes and "tune out" everything else while enacting a visualization exercise. When there *is* a distraction (God forbid), we feel it "grieves the Holy Spirit."

The result: Our focus in worship becomes idolatrous of perfect surroundings where the Spirit remains and hovers over our personal pew. Yikes! (Please understand that the Holy Spirit is not as unstable as we may think!) So here's the million-dollar question: Is personal, private spiritual euphoria at the top of God's agenda for congregational worship?

I am definitely to worship Him intimately in the privacy of my own pew, but hopefully not at the exclusion of the rest of the members.

3. To encourage ministry to the body

Romans 12:4–16 gives a clear picture of the basics of New Testament church life. Although instructions for life, many of the directives can be related to the corporate worship service as God joys in nurturing the community of believers.

Just as each of us has one body with many members, and these members do not all have the same function, so in Christ we who are many form one body, and each member belongs to all the others. We have different gifts, according to the grace given us. If a man's gift is prophesying, let him use it in proportion to his faith. If it is serving, let him serve; if it is teaching, let him teach; if it is encouraging, let him encourage; if it is contributing to the needs of others, let him give generously; if it is leadership, let him govern diligently; if it is showing mercy, let him do it cheerfully.

Love must be sincere. Hate what is evil; cling to what is good. Be devoted to one another in brotherly love. Honor one another above yourselves. Never be lacking in zeal, but keep your spiritual fervor, serving the Lord. *Be joyful in hope, patient in affliction, faithful in prayer. Share with God's people who are in need. Practice hospitality.*

Bless those who persecute you; bless and do not curse. Rejoice with those who rejoice; mourn with those who mourn. *Live in harmony with one another. Do not be proud, but be willing to associate with people of low position. Do not be conceited.*

—NIV, EMPHASIS ADDED

4. Repentance and transformation

When Isaiah saw the Lord seated on the throne, he was so overwhelmed by the glory and the majesty of the living God that he fell on his face, recognizing his uncleanness. (Read Isaiah 6:1–5.)

When we see the Lord for who He is, His penetrating light shines into the darkened areas of our souls and brings conviction. To see His holiness is to see our worthlessness without Him. The purity of Christ in all His glory reveals every blemish that humanity can name. Nothing is hidden from Him. If we're crying out for His presence and glory, it is imperative to realize what we're asking for. There is a legitimate work of repentance that must take place in our hearts before He can show us His fullness. Remember, it is His kindness that leads us to repentance.

The message of John the Baptist, and Jesus Himself, was simply, "Repent, for the kingdom is at hand." If we do not repent, we cannot experience God's kingdom. Jesus told Nicodemus that until he was born again, he couldn't even see the kingdom, let alone enter or experience it. He was trying to communicate that until a change of heart and mind transpires, one cannot even begin to comprehend the message of God's rule in their personal life or over the earth.

> ▲ We need a fresh
> ▲ view of His
> ▲ greatness and
> ▲ majesty before
> ▲ we can truly be
> ▲ changed into
> ▲ His likeness.

God wants to unveil our eyes in worship so we can see His kingdom—righteousness, peace and joy in the Holy Ghost. We need a fresh view of His greatness and majesty before we can truly be changed into His likeness. One way to begin is found in Paul's exhortation to the Romans:

> *Therefore, I urge you, brothers, in view of God's mercy, to offer your bodies as living sacrifices, holy and pleasing to God—this is your spiritual act of worship. Do not conform any longer to the pattern of this world, but be transformed by the renewing of your mind. Then you will be able to test and approve what God's will is—his good, pleasing and perfect will.*
>
> —ROMANS 12:1–2, NIV

Read 2 Timothy 1:9. Isaiah recognized how unclean he was in comparison to God's holiness. We can't be holy in our weak human flesh. How did the apostle Paul say we become holy?

_____

_____

▲▲▲▲▲▲▲

Read Isaiah 6:8. God cleansed Isaiah of his uncleanness, and the prophet was transformed. How did Isaiah respond to this transformation?

_____

_____

▲▲▲▲▲▲▲

When we present ourselves to God in worship, this act of repentance leads to the development of Christ's character in us. The essence of each worship response is a desire to be transformed by a superior power. Thus, the metamorphosis of the Spirit begins conforming us into the image of the Son as we behold Him. Looking at Jesus changes us into His likeness!

> *And we, who with unveiled faces all reflect the Lord's glory, are being transformed into his likeness with ever-increasing glory, which comes from the Lord, who is the Spirit.*
>
> —2 CORINTHIANS 3:18, NIV

5. Release the prophetic

Because God now makes His dwelling place with man, His voice is heard in the congregation of the saints.

> And I heard a loud voice from the throne saying, "Now the dwelling of God is with men, and he will live with them. They will be his people, and God himself will be with them and be their God."
>
> —Revelation 21:3, NIV

A story in the Bible about the prophet Elisha and a minstrel helps us to see how corporate worship can facilitate the release of a prophetic word. Joram, the king of Israel, Jehoshaphat, the king of Judah, and the king of Edom called on Elisha to give them a word from the Lord regarding their present circumstances. Elisha was unimpressed about being there, for he had no respect for the king of Israel. But he decided that he would stir up his gift out of respect for Jehoshaphat.

Looking at Jesus changes us into His likeness!

> Elisha said, "As surely as the LORD Almighty lives, whom I serve, if I did not have respect for the presence of Jehoshaphat king of Judah, I would not look at you or even notice you. But now bring me a harpist." While the harpist was playing, the hand of the LORD came upon Elisha.
>
> —2 Kings 3:14–15, NIV

As the harpist played, the spirit of the Lord came upon Elisha, and he spoke the word of the Lord to the three kings. Either Elisha simply liked good music to work by, or this illustrates a spiritual principle recorded for our education. In any case, the prophet was able to soothe his soul and stir up his spirit via the minstrel's music. Worship stimulates our spiritual sensitivity that we may hear His voice. Often the prophets are stirred during worship times to deliver the prophetic word. There's something about the worship of God that elevates our awareness of His presence and the voice of His Spirit.

In a later chapter, we will discover that the other gifts of the Spirit are also released through worship.

Read 1 Samuel 16:22–23. Even as a young man, David knew the power of worship. What happened when he played his harp and sang before King Saul?

_____

_____

▲▲▲▲▲▲▲

6. Warfare

The element of warfare in worship is a very strategic aspect. The fact that God judges His enemies through our praises is a fascinating phenomenon that many have tried to explain through the centuries. How does God use worship to take out vengeance on His foes? This also will be discussed in a later chapter.

7. Evangelism

Though our methods of outreach have changed or been modified over the centuries, the fact remains that the Great Commission is still indeed valid. People need the Lord, and whatever means used to share the living gospel is worthy of consideration. Worship can draw people into the kingdom!

▲▲

Worship stimulates our spiritual sensitivity that we may hear His voice.

▲▲

Graham Kendrick, noted for his pioneering work with praise marches on the streets of London and for the International Marches for Jesus, was speaking to a group of worship leaders in Dallas, Texas. Introducing the concept of the March for Jesus, he said, "People are not brought into the kingdom by mere miracles alone. Jesus did miracles, then they killed Him. They need a spiritual encounter with God."[3]

I remember participating in several Marches for Jesus over

the years. The onlookers, though overwhelmed by the number of people brave enough to profess Jesus on the streets of the city, were captivated by the exuberant and joyful praise. Many unbelievers have come into the kingdom by experiencing the presence of God through these marches. It's a graphic illustration of Jesus being lifted up and drawing all men to Himself (John 12:32).

When the people of the world *see* the relationship we have while worshiping the only true and living God, they are intrigued. Their spiritual curiosity is piqued, and we can actually become salt and light to them, pointing them to the Savior. Our relationship with Jesus uncovers their spiritual nakedness and reveals the lack of genuine fulfillment in their lives. Most do not realize that they lack any true meaning in their lives until they come face to face with the giver of life Himself. When He is granted permission to demonstrate His love, the emptiness of life seems to be even more intense in comparison to the fulfilling presence of God's all-consuming Being. The internal natural worship instinct is righted.

When the psalmist encountered God's intense demonstration of love, his response demonstrated this principle:

> *I waited patiently for the LORD; and He inclined to me and heard my cry. He brought me up out of the pit of destruction, out of the miry clay; and He set my feet upon a rock making my footsteps firm.* And He put a new song in my mouth, a song of praise to our God; many will see and fear, and will trust in the LORD.
>
> —PSALM 40:1–3, EMPHASIS ADDED

The song of praise draws attention.

> And I, if I be lifted up from the earth, will draw all men to Myself.
>
> —John 12:32

BLEST BE
THE TIE THAT BINDS

This hymn is rarely sung today, yet it captures the heart of God's longing for us to be in unity with our brothers and sisters in Christ. Perhaps we should reintroduce this song to twenty-first-century churches!

Blest be the tie that binds
Our hearts in Christian love;
The fellowship of kindred minds
Is like to that above.

Before our Father's throne
We pour our ardent prayers;
Our fears, our hopes, our aims are one,
Our comforts and our cares.

We share our mutual woes,
Our mutual burdens bear;
And often for each other flows
A sympathizing tear.[4]

> When the Word of God is in our hearts, it's easier for it to be on our lips.

PSALMS, HYMNS AND SPIRITUAL SONGS

Paul wrote to both the Ephesian and the Colossian churches to exhort, edify and admonish (correct) one another through the use of psalms, hymns and spiritual songs. (Read Ephesians 5:19; Colossians 3:16.) First he encouraged them to allow the Word of Christ to dwell in them richly. When the Word of God is in our hearts, it's easier for it to be on our lips. The power of the Word in worship through songs that reinforce the Scriptures increases faith to trust God for things we ordinarily may not believe for.

Often enough our worship times begin with thanksgiving, including testimonial songs of what God has done in our lives. When the direction of worship moves to confessions of our position in Christ because of what He's done for us, an edification or *building up of the body* transpires. This is accomplished through the medium of psalms, hymns and spiritual songs.

1. Psalms

The Book of Psalms has been referred to as the hymnbook or prayer book of the Bible. Though many contemporary churches have departed from the use of prayer books and liturgy as such, Psalms has been a useful tool in the order of worship for millennia. The psalmists have captured the struggles of life in a way that hundreds of generations have related to and benefited from.

The themes have a wide range of application to life. They include God's greatness and worth, salvation for the righteous, judgment for the wicked, conflict, resolution, internal questions of life, sin, repentance, forgiveness... and the list goes on. From passionate praise to recompensing injustice, each psalmist was able to write a song or poem to convey the heart's deepest emotion. Saints from all ages have found prescriptions for healthy worship in the pages of this ageless hymnbook.

These *poems of worship* contain a wealth of historical understanding concerning God's covenant with the people of Israel. The various psalmists incorporated excerpts of God's dealings into their musical repertoires. They would sing of how God brought them up out of the land of Egypt and destroyed their enemies. In the following stanzas they would sing of their forefathers' disobedience to God in the wilderness and tell of how God judged them as well. It was an important aspect of worship to remember both the goodness and the severity of God as they proclaimed His faithfulness.

Read Psalm 6:9. David poured out his heart honestly to God in prayer. What did he believe God would do with these prayers?

_____

_____

▲▲▲▲▲▲▲

Read Psalm 51:7–12. Some of the psalmists' songs were prayers of repentance. What happened when David repented for his sin?

_____

_____

▲▲▲▲▲▲▲

Read Psalm 95:6–7. Some psalms were an invitation to do what?

_____

_____

▲▲▲▲▲▲▲

As for aesthetics, the literary imagery portrayed in many of the psalms has contemporary significance and relevance for us. From the hearts of these writers comes true identification with human suffering. Encouragement is also available from those who have posed the same questions about life: "Where is God when I'm suffering?" Even from the noblest in the hall of faith comes this cry from the human heart, "If only the Lord would appear and defend my cause."

We cannot discount the humble prayer of the righteous man who implores God's judgment on His enemies. This proves still another purpose in the psalms that brings destruction to the forces of evil as a result of placing God in the place of supremacy. When the name of the Lord is exalted in a situation, the enemies of God are forewarned that "D-Day" is coming sooner or later! Though it may tarry, holy justice is displayed with a swift stroke of decision. It is simply this—blessing for the righteous and calamity for the wicked! We will look at this in a later chapter.

Today's praise and worship choruses will be tomorrow's hymns.

A powerful testimony to the validity of the psalms' current significance is in the fact that churches and synagogues around the world still use them today in their celebrations of worship. Whether it be from the call to worship, congregational songs, a responsive reading from a bulletin's order of service or the minister's declaration of the Word, there is rarely a service that goes by that doesn't contain some portion of a psalm.

A renowned pastor and professor of worship studies wrote, "Although Psalm-singing didn't become prominent in Israel until the time of Solomon's Temple, Psalm-singing as a form was used by the Mesopotamian Semitics. There are found numerous instances of Sumerian Psalms, Babylonian Psalms, Ugaritic Psalms and Egyptian Psalms."[5]

The roots of psalmody may be found in ancient civilizations, but recounting the history of faith and God's voice in worship can only be found in the psalms of the Bible. Along with an account of history, we've already looked at the patterns and methods for approaching God in worship that have been adhered to for centuries.

2. Hymns

Over the past generation, a criticism has arisen against the use of the hymnal in Charismatic or Free Praise churches. Understandably, many hymns from the seventeenth through the nineteenth centuries are more doctrinal and instructional than specifically praise or worship in their form. The language tends to be archaic, and the musical style is not contemporary. Many have associated hymn singing with dry and dead past religious experiences in their traditional background.

Yet the transition to a new type of corporate worship song has not been without resistance:

The debate is not a new one. A prominent American clergyman compiled the following ten reasons for opposing the new music trend of his day.

1. It's too new, like an unknown language.
2. It's not so melodious as the more established style.
3. There are so many new songs that it is impossible to learn them all.
4. This new music creates disturbances and causes people to act in an indecent and disorderly manner.
5. It places too much emphasis on instrumental music rather than on godly lyrics.
6. The lyrics are often worldly, even blasphemous.
7. It is not needed, since preceding generations have gone to heaven without it.
8. It is a contrivance to get money.
9. It monopolizes the Christian's time and encourages them to stay out late.
10. These new musicians are young upstarts and some of them are lewd and loose persons.

These ten reasons are adapted from a 1723 statement directed against the use of hymns! Some of these arguments are given today, but rather than being directed against hymns, they are now levied against contemporary Scripture and praise choruses.[6]

As you're probably beginning to realize, today's generation of praise and worship choruses will be tomorrow's generation of hymns. We must appreciate history in order to pursue destiny. What will our children think of our current worship music when they grow up? Creativity does continue! However, the viable use of hymns in a contemporary service is growing. The antiquated sound is being replaced with a more current style and some lyric changes that fit the current culture. Never underestimate the power of something old to spark an awareness of contemporary truth.

At the close of the infamous passage of parables, Jesus makes the following statement: "And He said to them, 'Therefore every scribe who has become a disciple of the kingdom of heaven is like a head of a household, who brings forth out of his treasure things new and old'" (Matt. 13:52).

Jesus compares the scribe to a skilful and faithful minister of the gospel. He is well versed in the things of God and is able to communicate them. He also compares him to a good master of a household who brings out fruit from last year's growth and this year's gathering, abundance and variety to entertain his friends. Old experiences and new observations all have their use. Daily we must review old lessons and learn new ones, too.

There is still value in my grandmother's life. She's not completely irrelevant because she's been in heaven for over fifteen years. Other than my parents, she was probably the single most spiritually influential person in my life while growing up. The rich heritage she left from her experiences throughout her eighty-three years still motivates me to seek the Lord and to follow Him wholeheartedly.

Wisdom says that I should pay attention to the ancient boundary stones she left behind that I might impart some of the same to my children and grandchildren. The old has value, provided I use it as a springboard toward my personal pursuit of God. I cannot build a tabernacle on information of the old thing alone and cause my worship to be constructed upon the simplicity of a nostalgic experience. I'm commissioned by God to search for Him in the newness of fresh revelation every day.

Ralph Martin, from the University of Sheffield, England, offers:

Historically, the singing of hymns to deity was an established practice in the Greco-Roman world long before the emergence of Christianity. Christian hymns differed from pagan hymnody, however, in celebrating a redemptive historical event; they have "prophetic" quality.[7]

On the heels of the American and French Revolutions in the middle to late 1700s came the Wesley brothers, preaching and singing throughout England. The Evangelical revival fervor that burned in their hearts would chart a new course of hymnology and church music for years to come and would radically change the flavor of Christian worship forever!

From a historical perspective, the development of Christian hymns is an incredible witness to the revival of holy desire in the church to express heartfelt worship to God in a way that was different from Latin liturgy. What has been called "The Golden Age of Hymns" exploded upon the world's scene not five hundred years ago, but less than two hundred fifty years ago. This is a relatively new worship phenomenon. The singing of hymns was not even officially approved in the Church of England until 1820. Of the 8,989 hymns contained in fifty-six collections by Charles and John Wesley, a good portion of those are still sung today.

The fact that many churches still use hymns of one form or another places them in a prophetic position. Declaring the resurrection of Jesus through hymn singing is an ageless prophetic statement. Unfortunately, some hymns, by their nature, are dated and are often seen as less important in our contemporary age of chorus singing. Because knowledge is increasing at such a rapid rate, songwriting is also increasing. But let us never forget the impetus hymns have given us in the pursuit of today's revelation of God!

> A spiritual song, originating from the Spirit, is given in order to edify, exhort or instruct the body.

3. Spiritual songs

The term *spiritual song* (in the Greek, *pneumatikos ode*—a supernaturally inspired or "God-breathed" melody), that is, "breathed or birthed by the Spirit," has readily been appropriated to any kind of spontaneously sung chant or motif of spiritual origin.[8] The *spiritual song* has also become known by other names such as *singing with the Spirit*, the *new song*, the *song of the Lord*, the *prophetic song* and the *selah*. The use of this form of song can be demonstrated in a variety of ways in the congregation.

> Charismatic congregations frequently sing in tongues, as Paul suggests in 1 Corinthians 14:15; such singing usually follows immediately after the congregation sings in the known language… Charismatics view the vocal praise song that wells up and flows from God's people as the voice of the Spirit of God in their midst, evidence of His life being released in the sanctuary and flowing out to bless the nations.[9]

Often a spontaneous song is lifted at a climactic point in worship, which is expressed by congregational singing in tongues (in the Spirit) or in a known language (in the understanding). This *new song*, as many call it, is regularly a precursor to some further prophetic expression. An individual may lift up his or her voice in song *to* the Lord or in a prophetic song *from* the Lord. In either case, the song, originating from the Spirit, is given in order to edify, exhort or instruct the body.

At times the song, sung by a solo voice, will be in the form of a love expression from the Bridegroom to the bride. Our response to that ought to be an expression of our love for Him in return—because God will respond to people who respond! At other times the song may be a confession prayer directly to God or a song exalting the name of the Lord with joy. Occasionally the song may come from the Psalms, expressing the predicament of a weary soul.

RISE UP

This chorus is a prophetic call to the church to fulfill its spiritual destiny. Songs like this release us to fulfill our corporate mission.

> Rise up, church of the living God.
> Let's seize the moment, our time has come.
> Rise up, soldiers of the cross.
> His Spirit leads us to reach out for the lost.

We will move beyond our fears, responding to Your voice in tears
Not our will but Yours be done.
We will be Your feet and hands, the fragrance of the Holy Lamb,
Through our lives Your love will come.

I set my face into the wind never to look back again.
Pressing on to win the prize.
These are days that we're a part of Your mighty move, O God.
Heaven's doors are open wide.[10]

In our pursuit of information and knowledge of God's purpose for corporate worship, it is critical for us to see the ultimate goal of David's tabernacle. It was not for the purpose of enjoying God's presence and hoarding the blessings. It was for God's dream to be realized. It was so the nations of the earth could gather before Him in worship. "'In that day I will raise up the fallen booth of David, and wall up its breaches; I will also raise up its ruins, and rebuild it as in the days of old; that they may possess the remnant of Edom and all the nations who are called by My name,' declares the Lord who does this" (Amos 9:11–12).

God's heart beats for the nations of the earth to encounter His presence and to know that He alone is God!

> God's heart beats for the nations of the earth to encounter His presence and to know that He alone is God!

LET'S TALK ABOUT IT

▲ Describe a time when God did something special in your life during a time of corporate worship.

_____

_____

▲▲▲▲▲▲▲

▲ What are the hindrances that keep people from entering into God's presence?

_____

_____

▲▲▲▲▲▲▲

▲ The Book of Psalms has been an encouragement to believers for centuries. What is your favorite psalm, and why?

_____

_____

▲▲▲▲▲▲▲

▲ Why is having the attitude of a servant integral to our worship experience?

_____

_____

▲▲▲▲▲▲▲

YOUR TIME WITH GOD

Father, I long to worship You more. I repent of and release anything I have been holding on to that could hinder me from fully entering into Your presence. I am overwhelmed by the fact that You desire to dwell with frail people such as me. I pray that as I abide in Your presence, You will transform me. My desire is to drink from the well of Your living water every day.

CHAPTER SIX

The Table of the Lord

IT WAS A WARM SUNNY DAY. The spring had brought new sights, sounds and smells to the little village of Cana located in the region of Galilee. *What a perfect day for a wedding,* Nathanael thought. This was his hometown, and he couldn't remember the weather ever being better. The journey from the region of Judea had been long and tiring, but it was good to be refreshed at home again.

Only a few days earlier Philip had called to him as he stood under a fig tree. Philip announced that they had found the One about whom the Law and the prophets spoke—the One was Jesus of Nazareth. Both skeptical and cynical, Nathanael said, "Can any good thing come out of Nazareth?" (Read John 1:43–49.) But after meeting Jesus and spending much time together on the road to Cana, Nathanael had a different outlook.

Jesus and His disciples were invited to a wedding, as was His mother, Mary. It was a typical Jewish celebration, with ceremony, festivities and lots of food and wine. (Read John 2:1–11.) As every good Jewish mother would be, Mary was concerned about how the wedding feast was progressing. After awhile she saw that the wine was running out, and she immediately kicked into "damage control mode." She told Jesus what was happening. Jesus said, "So what do you want Me to do about it? It's not time for Me to reveal My divinity!" But Mary took the bull by the horns and told the servants to do whatever Jesus said.

From a posture of internal purpose, and perhaps to humor His mother a bit, Jesus told the servants to fill the six water pots to the brim and to give a cup of the libation to the head-waiter. After tasting the water, which had become wine, the headwaiter called the bridegroom and said, "At parties, the

IN THIS CHAPTER YOU WILL DISCOVER THAT...

▲ The sacrificial body and blood of Christ—our covenantal meal—seals the New Covenant.

▲ The Passover meal gives us a picture to help us understand better the great sacrifice of our covenant Lamb—Jesus.

best wine is usually served first. Then after everyone is tipsy, the inferior quality wine is served and no one notices. But you have saved the best until last!" No one knew what had happened except the servants, Mary and the disciples. This was the first miracle in which Jesus displayed His glory, and the disciples believed in Him from that point!

Since marriage is the highest level of covenant into which two individuals can enter, it's fitting for the Master to perform His first miracle at a wedding feast. The apostle Paul tells us that the mystery of Christ and His church is epitomized in this union. By beginning His ministry at a wedding, Jesus made a strong statement about the future of the church. It was the initial invitation to join Him in covenant relationship through new wine. The prophetic picture of how much He wanted to be with us is embodied in the purchase agreement for our union with Him. It cost Him His life's blood! The invitation is now wide open to attend the ultimate Marriage Feast.

As we saw in an earlier chapter, it is not possible to approach the holiness of God without a holy sacrifice. There are several biblical illustrations of those who tried—with disastrous results. However, God made a way from the beginning so we would not be completely cut off from Him. Through the ages He looked for the fulfillment of the final covenant whereby we could come face to face with Him to discover His true heart for us, His bride.

COMING INTO COVENANT WITH GOD

A covenant is a contract or agreement between two parties. In the Old Testament the Hebrew word for *covenant, berith,* is derived from a root word that means "to cut." Consequently, a *covenant* is a "cutting," referring to the tradition of cutting or dividing animals into two parts when a covenant was initiated, with the contracting parties passing between the cut animals to make a covenant. (Read Genesis 15; Jeremiah 34:18–19.) The descriptive imagery is to say, "May God do to me what was done to this animal should I break this covenant."

Covenants or *oaths,* as is sometimes translated, were designed for establishing friendships that could be relied upon in case of war. Mutual protection was built into the agreement along with keeping peace and promoting commerce. The conditions of the covenant were clearly specified and confirmed by oaths. After they were written, sealed and ratified by the joining of hands, witnesses were called upon to offer credence to the act. Sometimes even God was called upon to witness the agreement.

When the act of sacrifice was made and the agreeing parties walked between the animal pieces, an altar was built and often named for the type of covenant that had just been cut. At times a customary tossing of salt would occur. Salt was often utilized in covenant making, probably symbolizing that which preserves and prevents decay. Such an act expressed hope that the covenant would endure. Then a gift exchange took place, followed by a feast that sealed the entire event. This covenantal meal was the final act of endorsement needed to seal the pact, and it provided an opportunity for agreeing parties to share together in fellowship.

When God entered into a covenant with Adam, Noah, Abraham, Isaac, Jacob, the nation of Israel, David and Jesus, His intent each time was to find a person or persons He could rely upon to accomplish His will in the earth. Because He so loved the earth and its inhabitants, He was determined to own it legally again. And Jesus, the covenant Lamb, ultimately purchased it back for God.

The New Covenant that God made with us is in the blood of Christ. In this chapter we will take a look at the significance of the sacrificial body and blood of Christ—our covenantal meal—that seals the New Covenant. Communion, our celebration of a covenant with God, is the final act of endorsement needed to seal God's covenant with man. It serves as an opportunity for the believer to share together with God in fellowship.

Read 1 Corinthians 1:9–10. Through Jesus, God brought us into close fellowship with Himself. This fellowship will flow over into what other area of our lives?

_____

_____

▲▲▲▲▲▲▲

Read 2 Corinthians 3:6. The New Covenant is not based on the letter of the Law, but on what?

_____

_____

▲▲▲▲▲▲▲

Read Psalm 89:34. What is God's promise regarding covenants He makes?

_____

_____

▲▲▲▲▲▲▲

> Communion, our celebration of a covenant with God, is the final act of endorsement needed to seal God's covenant with man.

God's request for intimate fellowship is as old as the earth itself. The theme of relationship is woven throughout the Scriptures and is particularly seen at meal times. In ancient cultures, sharing a meal was indicative of a deeper than casual relationship. Accepting an invitation to dinner acknowledged the pursuit of friendship. It showed that the invited guest approved of the host, the lifestyle of the host and his morals and principles.

Here are a few examples of God coming to dinner!

▲ *Exodus 24:9–11.* This is the fascinating story of Moses and the seventy elders meeting with God. After the Law was given, Moses instructed the young men to offer sacrifices to the Lord. Then God told Moses to bring the elders and come up to the mountain. When they came close to the mountain, "they saw the God of Israel; and under His feet there appeared to be a pavement of sapphire, as clear as the sky itself. Yet He did not stretch out His hand against the nobles of the sons of Israel; and they beheld God, and they ate and drank" (Exod. 24:10–11). This is a picture of a communion meal served by God Himself. As they ate and drank, they saw God! This does not mean that they simply "looked at" the Lord. They beheld Him; they perceived and contemplated His character. He pursued them to see what they would do. And when they responded to Him, He allowed them to stay for dinner.

▲ *John 4:7–38.* When Jesus was passing through the city of Sychar, He stopped at a well for a drink around lunchtime while His disciples went into town to buy food. While there He initiated a conversation with a morally questionable woman, offering her living water.

▲ *Luke 22:14–20.* On the night He was betrayed, Jesus observed the Passover meal with His disciples. During that time He revealed the final act of redemption, symbolizing it with the breaking of bread and sharing of the cup.

▲ *Luke 24:13–35.* After the Resurrection, as two men journeyed along the road to the town of Emmaus, they discussed their grief over the loss of Jesus. Suddenly Jesus appeared and began walking with them. As they spoke, Jesus instigated further discussion by reiterating messianic Scriptures to them. Arriving at their destination, Jesus acted as if He would continue to travel further, but the men pleaded with Him to stay. When they sat down for dinner, Jesus blessed the bread and broke it. Suddenly, their eyes were opened, and they recognized Him.

▲ *John 21:1–13.* The next day, Peter and some of the disciples were fishing on the Sea of Galilee. Still distraught over the crucifixion of Jesus, they resorted back to their previous occupation. After fishing all night, there still were no fish in the boat. About daybreak, someone standing on the shore shouted, "Cast your nets on the other side of the boat." To their amazement, their nets almost broke with an overflow of large fish. Just then, John said, "It's Jesus!"

Dumbfounded, they made their way back to shore as Jesus said, "The fire's hot; let's have breakfast!"

▲ *Acts 10:9–16.* A few years later in the city of Joppa, Peter was taking a nap about lunchtime, and the Lord spoke to him in a dream about taking the message of Christ to a Gentile man named Cornelius. God also wanted to have communion with Gentiles, and He employed Peter to preach the Good News.

▲ *Revelation 3:14–22.* Through John, Jesus spoke to the church at Laodicea. He rebuked them for their lukewarmness, lethargy and pride, making it clear that He disciplines those whom He loves. He then gave them an opportunity to repent and said, "Behold, I stand at the door and knock; if anyone hears My voice and opens the door, I will come in to him, and will dine with him, and he with Me" (Rev. 3:20). A famous picture of the Lord knocking on the door conjures up a "gentle Jesus" who asks permission to come inside the unbeliever's heart. That may be a reasonable rendition of what we've become comfortable with; however, Jesus' words to the church at Laodicea are more like a wake-up call to the church! Repent, and Jesus will come in and eat. That means He's willing to count the sin against us no longer. He will act as though His covenant was never broken!

▲ *Revelation 19:7–10.* In John's revelation, he sees the cosmic culmination of things to come in heaven and on earth. First the hallelujahs are raised—"Hallelujah! For the Lord our God, the Almighty, reigns" (v. 6). The next verses are about the marriage of the Lamb. "Blessed are those who are invited to the marriage supper of the Lamb" (v. 9). The final act of covenant consummation is the marriage feast, which Jesus inaugurated through His blood on the night of the Passover meal in Jerusalem. Because of His sacrifice, we can now celebrate the Eucharist as His bride, clothed in the fine linen of His righteousness, which is the wedding garment we wear when ruling with Him in heavenly places.

PSALM 116:12–19

This psalm foreshadows the table of the Lord with its reference to "the cup of salvation."

What shall I render to the LORD
For all His benefits toward me?
I shall lift up the cup of salvation,
And call upon the name of the LORD.
I shall pay my vows to the LORD,
Oh may it be in the presence of all His people.
Precious in the sight of the LORD
Is the death of His godly ones.
O LORD, surely I am Thy servant,
I am Thy servant, the son of Thy handmaid,
Thou hast loosed my bonds.
To Thee I shall offer a sacrifice of thanksgiving,
And call upon the name of the LORD.
I shall pay my vows to the LORD,
Oh may it be in the presence of all His people,
In the courts of the LORD's house,
In the midst of you, O Jerusalem.
Praise the LORD!

WHAT ARE PASSOVER AND COMMUNION ALL ABOUT?

The concept of a marriage union between God and His people can be traced back through the lineage of the patriarchs. This theme was proclaimed at the feast of Passover and is now applied to Jesus, the Bridegroom. Ideas of a messianic banquet can be found in both the Old and New Testaments. Eating and drinking in the kingdom of God is one of the best descriptions of communion.

The observance of communion is derived from the Jewish

feast of Passover. Jesus celebrated this as His last meal with the disciples. It parallels the New Covenant meal in many ways. Passover was one of three annual pilgrimage feasts and was celebrated on the fourteenth day of the month of Nisan (April in Western calendars). The purpose of the feast was to commemorate the deliverance of Israel from Egyptian bondage and the sparing of Israel when the destroyer struck the firstborn of Egypt.

Several days before the feast, the head of the household selected an unblemished lamb. On the evening of Passover, the lamb was slain, and its blood was sprinkled on the doorpost and lintel of the house where the family ate the meal. This signified that each family who did this was "covered" by the blood of that lamb against impending judgment. The lamb was roasted and served with unleavened bread and bitter herbs. The people were instructed to eat the meal dressed and ready to go.

Once the Hebrews developed their religious structure, built the tabernacle and established the priesthood, the Passover evolved in some ways. Now the lamb was to be slain at the entrance of the tabernacle rather than at home. The blood was to be sprinkled upon the brazen altar instead of the doorposts. Besides the family meal, national sacrifices were made every day during the Passover and the Feast of Unleavened Bread. Two other additions included the recitation of the history of the Passover and the singing of the Hallel (Ps. 113–118) during the meal.

The rich symbolism conveyed through the Passover meal is what Jesus used to make His point at the Last Supper. Ultimately Paul used more illustrations to communicate that Christ was the Passover Lamb. No longer do we need to fear God's wrath, because Jesus ratified the New Covenant with His own blood and removed the ultimate penalty of death for disobedience through forgiveness (Col. 2:14).

As New Covenant believers, the Passover holds much significance for us. Each part of it gives us a picture to help us understand better the great sacrifice of our covenant Lamb—Jesus.

> ... having canceled out the certificate of debt consisting of decrees against us and which was hostile to us; and He has taken it out of the way, having nailed it to the cross.
> —Colossians 2:14

1. The unblemished lamb represents Jesus, the Lamb of God, slain from the foundation of the world.

2. The blood of the lamb is a picture of Christ's blood poured out to cover and atone for the sins of the world.

3. The unleavened bread signifies His body without the yeast of sin's corruption.

4. The bitter herbs symbolize the suffering the Lord endured to purchase our deliverance.

5. The cup of salvation is the classic image of the entire sacrifice Jesus made.

> Jesus ratified the New Covenant with His own blood.

Read John 1:29. The Hebrew people understood the significance of sacrificing a lamb at Passover. How does this relate to what John the Baptist said about Jesus?

_____

_____

▲▲▲▲▲▲▲

Read Romans 6:23. Why is it important that Christ freed us from the bondage of sin?

_____

_____

▲▲▲▲▲▲▲

Read Revelation 12:10–11. The apostle John recorded that the power of the blood of the Lamb—Jesus—is important in doing what?

_____

_____

▲▲▲▲▲▲▲

When we partake of the Lord's Table we are celebrating the covenant Jesus made with us through His broken body and shed blood. The commemoration of this Christ event has varied in custom and practice around the world through the centuries. Worship traditions have survived by maintaining their usefulness—they are based on Scripture, and they pass the "prescription" for commemoration to the next generation. The terminology differs from place to place, and memories of the ordinance can evoke images of morbid past religious experiences, but partaking of the bread and the cup has had considerable significance for the church since Jesus first said it.

Paul received personal revelation of the importance of this communion experience from the Lord Himself, and he wanted to pass it along to the Corinthian church. He wrote about the significance of that first event when:

> *The Lord Jesus, on the night he was betrayed, took bread, and when he had given thanks, he broke it and said, "This is my body, which is for you; do this in remembrance of me." In the same way, after supper he took the cup, saying, "This cup is the new covenant in my blood; do this, whenever you drink it, in remembrance of me."*
>
> —1 CORINTHIANS 11:23–25, NIV

Every time we partake of the Table, we are to remember the Lord and proclaim His death until He comes.

Of the many "hard sayings" in the Bible, Jesus' statement about eating His flesh and drinking His blood is definitely one of them. After Jesus called Himself the "bread of heaven," the Jews began to argue among themselves. They could not grasp that Jesus was asking them to eat His flesh and drink His blood. They were well aware that the Law strictly forbade the consumption of blood. One who did such acts was to be "cut off from his people" (Lev. 7:27).

> *Jesus said to them, "I tell you the truth, unless you eat the flesh of the Son of Man and drink his blood, you have no life in you. Whoever eats my flesh and drinks my blood has eternal life, and I will raise him up at the last day. For my flesh is real food and my blood is real drink. Whoever eats my flesh and drinks my blood remains in me, and I in him."*
>
> —JOHN 6:53–56, NIV

The Lord was attempting to completely mess up their theology. They were thinking about the physical ramifications only and "choked" on the truth. Even His disciples had difficulty with these words. Knowing they were offended, Jesus continued, "The Spirit gives life; the flesh counts for nothing. The words I have spoken to you are spirit and they are life" (John 6:63, NIV).

> When we partake of the Lord's Table we are celebrating the covenant Jesus made with us through His broken body and shed blood.

The spiritual implication of eating His flesh and drinking His blood has to do with the words He spoke to them. *Partaking of His flesh and blood* is the same concept as *abiding in the vine.* Believers feed on Christ's body and blood, not with our literal mouth, but by faith in our soul. Faith becomes the mouth of the soul. By the power of the Holy Spirit, we do this not only in our observance of the Lord's Supper, but whenever faith in Him is exercised. Obeying His commandments keeps us in Christ, where we feed on His words, which are true spirit and life.

> Faith becomes the mouth of the soul.

Read Leviticus 17:11. Why is the shedding of blood in sacrifice such a significant symbol that God wants us to understand?

_____

_____

▲▲▲▲▲▲▲

Read Hebrews 9:13–15. The author of Hebrews mentions one of the works the shedding of Christ's blood accomplished. What is it?

_____

_____

▲▲▲▲▲▲▲

LET US BREAK BREAD TOGETHER

This is one of many famous hymns written to celebrate the holy moment of the Lord's Supper. Churches today would do well to recapture the beauty of communion at the Lord's Table.

Let us break bread together on our knees;
Let us break bread together on our knees.

When I fall on knees with my face to the rising sun,
O Lord, have mercy on me.

Let us drink the cup together on our knees;
Let us drink the cup together on our knees.[1]

MEETING THE LORD AT HIS TABLE

The Old Testament priests were to place unleavened shew-bread on the table in the tabernacle. The word *shewbread* literally means "the bread of face," or "the bread of the presence." It speaks of an encounter with God—seeing Him, knowing Him, being fed by Him. The shewbread was a prophetic picture of one day standing face to face with God and being nourished by His spiritual words of life through the communion supper!

Jesus commanded that we observe the Lord's Table for several reasons:

1. *To commemorate His death.* "Do this… in remembrance of Me" (1 Cor. 11:25). It is a celebration to recall Christ's sacrificial death and anticipate His coming again in judgment. Jesus told His followers to continue the practice "in remembrance of Me." This is not just a passionate memory of a past event. By recalling Christ's sacrificial death we make it a reality again, thus increasing the awareness of the Lord's presence.

2. *To seal and realize the benefits of the New Covenant.* Through this rite, Jesus endorses His promises to His people as they solemnly consecrate themselves to Him and to His service. This is the New Covenant in the blood of Christ—the Old Covenant was broken by unfaithful Israel. The cup, representing the blood, enacts the covenant, and the whole meal ratifies it. This also speaks of God's rule in establishing something new in the kingdom of God. The prophet Isaiah lists what Jesus came to do for us: "Surely he *took up our infirmities* and *carried our sorrows,* yet we considered him stricken by God, smitten by him, and afflicted. But he was *pierced for our transgressions,* he was *crushed for our iniquities; the punishment that brought us peace was upon him, and by his wounds we are healed*" (Isa. 53:4–5, NIV, emphasis added).

3. *To encourage the relationship of intimacy through communion with Christ.* The apostle Peter shares these words, "For by these He has granted to us His precious and magnificent promises, in order that by them you might become partakers of the divine nature, having escaped the corruption that is in the world by lust" (2 Pet. 1:4).

4. *To promote the fellowship of communion with believers.* "Since there is one bread, we who are many are one body; for we all partake of the one bread" (1 Cor. 10:17).

The elements used to represent Christ's body and blood are bread and wine. The kind of bread, whether leavened or unleavened, is not specified. Jesus used unleavened bread simply because it was on the Passover meal table at that moment. Wine was specified as the correlation between blood and the fruit of the vine. (Read Matthew 26:26–29.) Depending on personal convictions, some prefer to use grape juice as a wine substitute.

In summary, by partaking of the Table, we partake of Jesus Himself, all that He is and all He has accomplished to make us wholly His. Eating the bread depicts a consuming of His broken body, which brings healing to the body and soul. As the prophet Isaiah declares in the earlier passage, Jesus was beaten with whips in order to purchase healing for us. Partaking of the Bread of Heaven can drive out infirmity.

As Isaiah also mentions, Jesus was pierced for our transgressions. Every bit of our disobedience was laid upon Him. He was crushed and bruised for iniquitous sinful habit patterns—even those passed down from our forefathers. And the punishment He received was for the purchase of our peace! Drinking the cup releases New Covenant life in forgiveness of sin and breaking the bondage of its power. Deliverance can occur, and overwhelming peace can replace the emotional sense of despair in the wounded heart.

Expect the miraculous when actions are combined with faith at the Lord's Table.

From the earliest writings, it was understood that the risen

Christ Himself was present at this meal in the form of bread and wine. However, in the earliest eras, this "presence" was not explained philosophically. In later centuries, more writings began to proclaim the natural and supernatural, earthly and heavenly combination of the elements. The amalgamation of mystical and ethereal ideas of the elements caused them to take on seemingly "magical" powers.

Around the thirteenth century, the Roman Catholic Church, in an effort to defend their biblically grounded faith conviction, attempted to explain conceptually what is called *the real presence of Christ.* The church believed Christ was really present in this ordinance, and His presence implies real change. Therefore, substantial changes in material beings were present. Likened to the Incarnation where the Word became flesh by the power of the Spirit, so the risen Lord takes up the bread and wine by the power of the Spirit as a means of a manifestation of His real presence.

Soon the doctrine of transubstantiation was promulgated, teaching that the bread literally became the body of the Lord Jesus, and the wine was supernaturally transformed into the blood of Christ. At certain points in history, this doctrine was so intensely taught that the church's members were held in fear. If the people were not pliable to local leadership, they could be denied the Eucharist. Salvation qualities were attributed to the elements themselves, which began to provoke the mysterious nature by which it was administered and received.

In the late fifteenth century, Martin Luther took Rome to task over the celebration of the entire Catholic mass. He felt that the mass had become a particular kind of work by which the people pled for God's favor through the performance of a religious ceremony. He also believed that the Lord's Supper had become a ceremonial work to gain points with God instead of an exercise of faith. He implied that the mass erroneously presented the Lord's Supper as a sacrifice (sacrament) only, given to God instead of being a benefit given from God that is received by faith. The classic Lutheran position on the rite of the Lord's Table states that the true body and blood of Christ are present in, with and under the elements of bread and wine. And this Presence exists through the power of God's Word, which promises His presence when the elements are received ("This is My body…").

HERE IS BREAD, HERE IS WINE

This song by Graham Kendrick reminds us of a simple and yet profound truth—that it was the broken body of Jesus and His shed blood that restored us to fellowship with the Father.

In this bread there is healing,
In this cup there's life forever,
In this moment by the Spirit,
Christ is with us here.

Here is bread, here is wine.
Christ is with us, He is with us.
Break the bread, drink the wine,
Christ is with us here.

Here we are joined in one.
Christ is with us, He is with us.
We'll proclaim 'til He comes,
Jesus crucified.[2]

OBSERVANCE OF COMMUNION

Through history, the ceremonial observance of the Lord's Table has included different methods and even terms. Today this observance is recognized by a number of terms. These include:

1. *The Eucharist.* Used by liturgical churches, this term literally means "thanksgiving." The term *eucharist* comes from the blessing pronounced over the bread and wine, referring to Jesus' blessing the Father before the elements were distributed to the disciples. This observance underlines Christ's sacrificial death as a cause for thanksgiving to God.

2. *Communion.* This term is used more in fundamental and evangelical churches, and it stresses the sharing in

Christ's blood and body, which makes believers one. (Read 1 Corinthians 10:16–17.) There are three aspects of the term *communion* with regard to fellowship:

▲ Fellowship with God (Read Genesis 18:17–33.)
▲ Fellowship between Christ and His people (Read John 14:23.)
▲ Fellowship of believers with one another (Read Ephesians 4:1–6.)

3. *The Lord's Supper.* This term highlights Christ's role as the Host and the One who invites us to dine. Paul used this term to describe the nature of the Lord's Supper. Consequently, it is the expression used by many churches to refer to their celebration of Jesus' final, memorial meal with His disciples. The *Lord's Supper,* or the *Lord's Table,* is so called because there is fellowship between Christ and His disciples, and of the disciples with one another. (Read 1 Corinthians 10:16–17.)

4. *The breaking of bread.* The Book of Acts refers to this worship event as the "breaking of bread" (Acts 2:42, 46; 20:7). Some have interpreted this to mean regular shared meals, while others see this as the covenantal meal of communion.

5. *Koinonia.* Paul used the Greek term *koinonia* to express the basic meaning of the Christian faith as a sharing in the life and death of Christ. This creates an intimate relationship between Jesus and the believer. The believers create intimacy in relationship with one another through partnership or unity. Paul reiterates that we are one body (1 Cor. 10:17).

6. *The cup of blessing.* Paul also spoke of the Lord's Supper in terms of its component parts:
▲ The "cup of blessing" (Read 1 Corinthians 10:16.)
▲ The "cup of the Lord" (Read 1 Corinthians 10:21.)
▲ The "table of the Lord" (Read 1 Corinthians 10:21.)

> Since there is one bread, we who are many are one body; for we all partake of the one bread.
> —1 Corinthians 10:17

7. *Bread of Heaven.* Jesus referred to Himself as *food:* "I am the bread of life. Your fathers ate the manna in the wilderness, and they died. This is the bread which comes down out of heaven, so that one may eat of it and not die" (John 6:48–50).

The following is a format used in traditional liturgy when celebrating the Table. Prior to receiving the Lord's Supper, the hymn *"Sanctus"* ("Holy, Holy, Holy") is sung, articulating the wonder and adoration of all creatures before the Creator. It is sung with heaven and earth in mind, as each declares the glory of God respectively and in unity.

The second part of the hymn is taken from Psalm 118, which addresses the festival sacrifice. It concludes with a cry for deliverance, acclaiming, "Hosanna, save us!" and "Blessed is He who comes in the name of the Lord!" This is the greeting to Him who comes to the Table in the form of the bread and the cup. The theology of thought encompasses the worship of almighty God and the manifested Son, our Deliverer. During the hymn, the celebrant (officiator) prepares the articles for the Table.

In all Christian traditions, prayer accompanies the receiving of the elements, though the form and content may vary. The *Eucharistic prayer* is often called the prayer of consecration and has essentially two themes: 1) thanksgiving to God for His acts of creation and redemption in Christ through which He demonstrated His love for us, and 2) an invocation of the Holy Spirit on the congregation and on the gifts of the bread and wine.

As the celebrant elevates the consecrated bread and cup respectively, the blessings are pronounced in the *Words of Institution.* These are typically the words used by Jesus when He established the ordinance of the supper. As is the tradition in most liturgical, evangelical and Charismatic churches, the celebrant quotes Paul's interpretation of the story from 1 Corinthians 11:23–26.

When the words "This is My body" and "This is My blood" are spoken, the congregation joins in the proclamation, "Christ has died. Christ has risen. Christ will come again!"

The rudimentary core of faith rests on these three statements.

The prayer continues as the congregation declares the celebration of the memorial sacrifice of thanks for Christ's death, resurrection and ascension, offering "these gifts" (the bread and wine) and themselves as worship to God.

Read Romans 6:5–6. Why is it important to identify with the death of Christ?

_____

_____

▲▲▲▲▲▲▲

Read 1 Corinthians 15:17–20. Why did the apostle Paul say the resurrection of Jesus from the dead was so important?

_____

_____

▲▲▲▲▲▲▲

The next part is the *calling down upon.* Here the Holy Spirit is asked to come upon the elements and the people so that what is intended when God's people meet at His Table will, in fact, occur. Prayers ascend for the revelation of Christ in the bread and cup to supercede earthly realms of understanding. At this point, the *Lord's Prayer* is recited together.

▲▲▲

We must be broken for the world that they might find life in His name.

▲▲▲

The breaking of bread is done in the sight of all the people. *Fraction* is the liturgical term used for breaking the bread. This is sometimes done during the *Words of Institution,* or it can occur during the singing of a hymn. The fraction is a visual and even audible experience and can be very effective when the congregation is served from a single loaf broken apart for distribution. It symbolizes Christ being broken for us that we might have life. And now we must be broken for the world that they might find life in His name.

Another dimension of revelation is anticipated at the breaking of the bread. Just as the eyes of the disciples on the

Emmaus road after the Resurrection were opened, Jesus is often expected to open the eyes of His people that they may know Him in the power of His resurrection and the fellowship of His sufferings (Phil. 3:10).

Read 1 Corinthians 11:24. For what reason did Jesus say His body would be broken?

_____

_____

▲▲▲▲▲▲▲

Read 1 Corinthians 10:17. What did the apostle Paul say happens when people from all different races and backgrounds partake of the bread of Christ's body?

_____

_____

▲▲▲▲▲▲▲

In historic liturgies, the hymn *"Agnus Dei"* ("Lamb of God") is sung during the breaking of the bread or during the distribution of the gifts. If the celebrant is serving the elements, the people come forward and kneel to receive. For the service of the bread, "The Body of Christ, the Bread of Heaven" is pronounced. And for the service of the cup, "The Blood of Christ, the Cup of Salvation" is given. The appropriate response is then, "Amen."

Most of you reading this book are probably not attending a strongly liturgical church. However, the rich heritage developed and passed down from these historical churches is what has fueled the flame of contemporary revival. Some view tradition as dead and dry, while others see it as connecting to something tried and true and worthy of investigating. Many have wanted more from their experience at the Lord's Table than just a good feeling. Whatever your spiritual view, never underestimate the power of strong biblical truth as displayed through historical means. God can still speak.

There is one last point regarding communion that I believe is absolutely essential to absorb. It is in regard to partaking in an unworthy manner. Having heard the term since childhood,

> That I may know Him, and the power of His resurrection and the fellowship of His sufferings, being conformed to His death.
> —Philippians 3:10

I usually feared that I was not performing well enough to partake of the elements along with the rest of the "perfect" saints. But the requirements go a bit deeper than a matter of simply being flawless in heart attitude and character. The only passage of Scripture we find these cautions is in Paul's first letter to the Corinthian church. This passage outlines the deeper requirements:

1. *Celebrating the Table of the Lord should be done with honesty and integrity.* Paul addresses issues of immorality in the church and advises the Corinthians to "clean out the old leaven, that you may be a new lump, just as you are in fact unleavened. For Christ our Passover also has been sacrificed. Let us therefore celebrate the feast, not with old leaven, nor with the leaven of malice and wickedness, but with the unleavened bread of sincerity and truth" (1 Cor. 5:7–8).

2. *Partakers of the Table must be wholly separate to God.* When addressing issues of food sacrificed to demons, Paul makes the following statement: "You cannot drink the cup of the Lord and the cup of demons; you cannot partake of the table of the Lord and the table of demons" (1 Cor. 10:21).

3. *Self-examination is commanded before partaking of the elements.* "A man ought to examine himself before he eats of the bread and drinks of the cup. For anyone who eats and drinks without recognizing the body of the Lord eats and drinks judgment on himself. That is why many among you are weak and sick, and a number of you have fallen asleep. But if we judged ourselves, we would not come under judgment" (1 Cor. 11:28–31, NIV).

When Paul speaks of "recognizing the body of the Lord" or properly "discerning the body," he was not speaking about the once-dead cadaver of Jesus. He was speaking about "the body of Christ," which is the people of God in a particular location.

The matter of relationship divisions in the church and poor manners of etiquette needed addressing. Apparently certain individuals would bring their supper to church and eat in front of others who were less fortunate. And from this passage we read that others would come to church and get drunk on the wine they brought from home. These folks had either lost or never really found the true meaning of the Lord's Table.

To eat of the Lord's Supper in an "unworthy manner" involves, in part, factions or cliques, which show contempt for the poor who are also part of the body of Christ. The unworthy partaker is then guilty of the body and blood of the Lord and is visited with judgments from God because he cannot properly appreciate the rest of the body of Christ. (Read 1 Corinthians 11:21–22, 27, 29–30.)

Paul put his foot down and told them to repent, reconcile and not bring their dinner or their bottle to church anymore. The focus of the meeting was now going to be on the Table of the Lord and what God wanted to do in their gatherings.

This is strangely similar to what we've been discussing in these chapters. Being aware of what God is doing among the whole body is what communion is all about. It's not only about me taking care of private business with God. The writer to the Hebrews sums this up nicely when speaking about the way of worship the New Covenant affords. There is a strong sense of purity in conjunction with unity among the body.

Therefore, brothers, since we have confidence to enter the Most Holy Place by the blood of Jesus, by a new and living way opened for us through the curtain, that is, his body, and since we have a great priest over the house of God, let us draw near to God with a sincere heart in full assurance of faith, having our hearts sprinkled to cleanse us from a guilty conscience and having our bodies washed with pure water. Let us hold unswervingly to the hope we profess, for he who promised is faithful. And let us consider how we may spur one another on toward love and good deeds. Let us not give up meeting together, as some are in the habit of doing, but let us encourage one another—and all the more as you see the Day approaching.

—HEBREWS 10:19–25, NIV, EMPHASIS ADDED

LET'S TALK ABOUT IT

▲ Explain how understanding the death and resurrection of Jesus Christ has made a personal impact on you.

_____

_____

▲▲▲▲▲▲▲

▲ Why is it important to examine our hearts before we take communion?

_____

_____

▲▲▲▲▲▲▲

▲ What about the observance of communion is most meaningful to you?

_____

_____

▲▲▲▲▲▲▲

▲ What does entering into a covenant with Christ teach us about our relationships with one another?

_____

_____

▲▲▲▲▲▲▲

YOUR TIME WITH GOD

Father, thank You for providing a way, through Jesus' death and resurrection, to enter into a covenant relationship with You. Thank You for inviting me to eat at Your table and to fellowship with You. Jesus, I am in awe of the sacrifice You made by allowing Your body to be broken and Your blood to be spilled for my sake. Take away my sin and my shame. Help me to walk in unity with my brothers and sisters in Christ, who share in this covenant relationship.

CHAPTER SEVEN

Playing Skillfully

THERE WERE ABOUT FORTY-FIVE PEOPLE PRESENT IN THE LITTLE COUNTRY CHURCH OFF RURAL HIGHWAY 38. Most were farmers and field workers whose families had lived in the area for years. Each family had passed the farm down to the next generation for over a century. It was a quaint community with nearly two thousand in population.

The worship service began with the old familiar song "Power in the Blood." The band, consisting of a piano, guitar, a tambourine and Johnny's clarinet, played with all their might in praise to God as the people joyously joined in singing some hymns and praise choruses. The only real distraction was Sister Anna's tambourine. She had a hard time with rhythm, and staying on the beat was next to impossible for her. It was difficult for her to hear the rest of the band because she sat toward the rear of the room. But her heart was pure and in the right place.

The special music was a clarinet solo with piano accompaniment. Johnny needed the practice before his elementary school band performed in concert, and he loved playing his clarinet for the Lord. The congregation sat with smiles on their faces while Johnny played his selection during the offertory, then applauded with vigor as the youngster took a bow and sat down amidst comments of, "Oh, how sweet," and "Isn't he progressing well?"

At the same time, fifty miles down the interstate, more than three thousand worshipers gathered for the second service in the newly completed Family Worship Center. Many of the members were doctors, lawyers or teachers—even two local legislators attended on a semiregular basis. The expectations of the people were high as they gathered for worship

IN THIS CHAPTER YOU WILL DISCOVER THAT...

▲ Music is a vehicle for worship that has been used in worship since the time of David's tabernacle.

▲ As musicians in the kingdom of God, we have a mandate from the Lord to make His praise glorious.

▲ Leading worship is taking the congregation to a place where they are introduced to God's menu and agenda.

that morning. The previous week the pastor had informed them that they were to have a special musical guest the next weekend.

State-of-the-art equipment and audiovisual gear were maximized in the extremely twenty-first-century structure situated on prime property in a very affluent section of town. The orchestra and robed choir were prepared with an opening song: "We've Come to Praise Him." There was no need to invite the people to stand, as everyone was on their feet before the introduction had concluded. The excellence of quality was seen in the professional presentation. Hands were lifted, bodies were swaying and hearts were expressing worship with unabashed abandon.

Music is a vehicle for worship.

A harpist ministered the special music with a seventeenth-century instrument that she had restored herself. The congregation sat in awe. With a master's degree in performance from a prestigious music school and a position in the local symphony orchestra, her gift and talent were in demand around the state. The performance was flawless!

After the applause of the congregation subsided, the pastor preached a dynamic sermon about "Life in the Fast Lane With Jesus." It was certainly a well-polished service of worship that had both traditional and contemporary appeal.

Here are two different expressions of worship in two totally different environments. With which do you think the Lord was more pleased? That decision would be like comparing apples to oranges. It would not be reasonable to make that judgment based on such a limited scope of knowledge. A relevant question would be, "Did each community of believers make their best effort to worship God wholeheartedly with what they had?"

As I see it, an issue of concern presents itself in each scenario. The smaller church has few options with regard to musicians and musicianship. Often, whoever can play the guitar or the piano with any degree of dexterity is voted hands down to lead the musical portion of the worship service. Many churches are just happy to have some musical accompaniment.

Yet on the other side of the coin, some larger churches have a similar problem. Over the last half century, the "paid professional" mentality in the larger church has caused the congregation to abdicate her role of viable interaction with God in worship. In some places, those with the most talent, proficiency and degrees are placed up front to lead others in worship simply because of their skill, with little regard for character, lifestyle or commitment to Christ.

In both settings, it's possible for those who play and sing to hold the rest of the church hostage with their sensitive attitudes or creative natures. Though many musicians have mastered their propensity toward melancholy emotions, others tend to be insecure about their talents and need consistent reinforcing. Another more prominent character issue is that of the "prima donna." If things are not exactly to their liking, they will sometimes take their toys and go home. I've heard it said, "Trying to manage creative people is like trying to herd cats!" As a musician and worship leader for many years, I can testify to this as a fact! But let's take a look at what the Word has to say about skill and its relativity to worshiping the Lord.

THE ROLE OF MUSIC IN WORSHIP

To begin, we must establish that music by itself is not worship. Music is a *vehicle* for worship that has typically been used in the observance of religious rites for millennia. The importance of music in worship to God dates back to the time of the Exodus when Miriam sang and danced the deliverance song on the banks of the Red Sea. However, the regular use of music and instruments in worship is not regularly seen until the time of David's tabernacle. Though many of David's songs, which were written in his youth, are recorded in the Book of Psalms, their public use is not recorded until years after their writing.

Perhaps you've heard music and its use for worship discussed in terms of what is sacred, secular or satanic. Many examples could be given to illustrate the differences. Music, in and of itself, is amoral—neither holy nor unholy, neither right nor wrong, neither good nor bad. What gives music its nature is the way it is used and by whom it is performed. Since music is but a vehicle for exaltation and has no mind of its own, it serves the purpose of its creator—positively or negatively.

In Old Testament times, music was considered a part of life. It wasn't dichotomized into sacred or secular compartments. There were songs for planting and songs for harvest. There were songs for birthing, dying, peace, war, celebration and worship. Music was never disassociated from the ebb and flow of natural events. It was viewed as the language of the heart and seen as intrinsic to the human soul.

Because the Bible says, "Let everything that has breath praise the LORD" (Ps. 150:6), the methods or vehicles we use to do so are subject to the individual who is offering praise. And with their breath (or all their being) they use varied instruments to give thanks. The Book of Psalms is filled with references regarding the use of brass, woodwinds, strings, percussion instruments and voices to praise God. Part of the culture was to "move" to the music, as is apparent in Psalm 150.

> Praise the LORD! Praise God in His sanctuary; praise Him in His mighty expanse. Praise Him for His mighty deeds; praise Him according to His excellent greatness. Praise Him with trumpet sound; praise Him with harp and lyre. Praise Him with timbrel and dancing; praise Him with stringed instruments and pipe. Praise Him with loud cymbals; praise Him with resounding cymbals. Let everything that has breath praise the LORD. Praise the LORD!
>
> —Psalm 150

Read Psalm 28:7. There are many occasions for worshiping the Lord in song. What is one of the reasons David gave for singing praises?

_____

_____

▲▲▲▲▲▲▲

Read Psalm 98:1. What type of song are we to sing to the Lord?

_____

_____

▲▲▲▲▲▲▲

Read Exodus 15:20–21. It is appropriate to praise God by singing when He delivers us from the enemy. About what event did the prophetess Miriam sing a song of victory?

_____

_____

▲▲▲▲▲▲▲

Many instruments mentioned in the Bible were creations of ancient civilizations and were shared or borrowed from other cultures. Numerous instruments we use today are derivatives of these ancient prototypes. A number of these were percussion instruments that have evolved through the centuries. For example, the original tambourine (*tof*) was initially designed without jingles and was used as a small drum for rhythm.

A natural sense of timing is inherent in the human structure. Rhythm is found at the core of every culture. The expression of natural rhythm is almost always communicated by way of percussive instruments. This runs contrary to the thinking of many who believe that drums are the inspiration of Satan. One of the facts that has seemed to support this presupposition about drums is the knowledge that tribal peoples have used drums and percussion instruments in ritualistic worship of false gods for centuries.

But, as biblical history confirms, the Law God gave to Moses had several hundred rules and regulations instructing the people of Israel how NOT to behave like the pagan nations around them. Yet none of the laws have any mention forbidding certain types of music or musical styles. We can deduce from historical accounts that the instruments and music the Hebrews used were the same or similar in style to those of their neighbors. The difference in the worship arena was that the instruments the Hebrews used were used to glorify God in celebration.

Christians have always seemed to have an uneasy time with percussion and rhythm. But rhythm is nothing more than mathematics. With today's musical technology you can program virtually any beat or rhythm into a computer simply by entering numbers. It's nothing more than numbers. Are some numbers more holy than other numbers? How ridiculous is that? The body was constructed by God to enjoy the feeling of rhythm. The heart beats in rhythm. The seven-day cycle of activity and rest is all about rhythm. The more you feel in your body the more alive you are. To not feel rhythm is to be dead.[1]

The same is true about vocabulary use in language. Words are not separated into sacred and secular categories. Even the New Testament was written in everyday Greek—not classical Greek. Words used in biblical writings were the same words spoken by many pagans throughout the Roman Empire. It was not the words themselves that were sacred or secular, but the message they communicated.

It is not clear how ancient music sounded, as there are no recordings or firsthand accounts recalling the ancient cultural and linguistic affectations. But biblical evidence proves that music was not an art intended to showcase the skill of the performer or to draw attention to the composer. Musical skill was encouraged and admired as a craft, but it was subservient to the purpose of the event that it accompanied. Fans did not attend concerts just to hear music performed. Even when performed by professionals, music was intended to assist the whole community in celebration.

▲▲

Music and art are God's gifts to restore the soul—not to destroy it.

▲▲

This is not to say that musical concerts given by today's professionals are evil or that they are misleading the current generation away from the goal of music. Nonsense! Music and art are vehicles for communication. But what is the message that's being communicated? As the artists artistically express their craft, they convey their personal sense of significance in life through the medium of interpretive art. Listeners and viewers are welcomed into the artists' world to experience their message, and then given an opportunity to respond with either "Bravo" or "Boo"!

What makes an artist's expression holy or profane? It is what the artist chooses to exalt. Is it self-indulgence through carnal lusts, sexual perversion, power, greed, anger and vengeance? Or is it the message of hope for the condition of human frailty? Does it draw attention to itself, or is it pointing to a viable solution for a universal dilemma? Consider this: Music and art are God's gifts to restore the soul—not to destroy it.

As musicians in the kingdom of God, we have a mandate from the Lord to make His praise glorious (Ps. 66:2). We do this by offering our best to Him. What we are and what we have is our gift to God. By definition, to *excel* is to move beyond a proper limit. And *excellence* is a surpassing feature or virtue. So the pursuit of excellence is found in offering what we have and finding ways to increase the measure of its value.

Read 1 Peter 4:10. Why is it important to offer our best to the Lord?

_____

_____

▲▲▲▲▲▲▲

Read Psalm 56:13. What is one reason David gave for why we have such great cause to celebrate the Lord in praise?

_____

_____

▲▲▲▲▲▲▲

In many churches, the philosophy of worship creates an open door policy of "Ya'll come." Anyone who plays any kind of instrument or expresses in any kind of artistic way is welcome to be a part of the worship team. Some have had lessons; some haven't. Some are skilled; some aren't. Among the many arguments, one question has often been posed, "Should we let these people play or sing?" Well, do you *know* them, or do you simply *need* them? The old adage "You can't tell a book by its cover" is very applicable.

Another philosophy is to audition everyone who desires to participate in the music and arts ministry formally. The

Sing the glory of His name; make His praise glorious.
—Psalm 66:2

audition process may be intimidating, especially when vying for one of the three first-soprano positions left in the choir or for the duet dance in the Christmas program. The scrutiny for talent can be intense either because of a performance spirit or because of the church's vision.

There are some legitimate questions to consider, including, "Who is our target audience?" "To whom are we ministering?" and "What are we hoping to accomplish?" These answers will help to identify the purpose behind the worship team's activities because the core beliefs for the team—and the church—will be reinforced by the actions of the team as it ministers.

What is it about excellence that pleases the Lord most? The greatest quality of excellence is demonstrated by the desire to increase the capacity of the container. If we can hold more of God's glory, we can give out more! As we've seen through Scripture in previous chapters, God is not enamored by talented, gifted or charismatic personalities. He wants humble and teachable hearts that He can use to accomplish the goal of touching His people. Not only does He want to fill us up—He wants to flow through us as open and prepared channels.

Pursuing excellence is not a gerbil's wheel performance for an occasional pat on the back and the accompanying, "Atta boy"! Nor is it the rigorous training that precedes a dog and pony show. For all of us—including creative and gifted individuals—the most important quality of a consecrated communicator is the heart attitude. It is vitally important to consider honestly our intentions and objectives for performing in the house of the Lord so as not to confuse *performance* or *perfection* with *ministry.*

Speaking to leaders, the apostle Paul said, "And we beseech you, brethren, to know them which labour among you, and are over you in the Lord, and admonish you" (1 Thess. 5:12, KJV). If the worship team is "up in front" of the people, they can be considered leaders in that arena. We are instructed to "know them," or to pay attention to their lifestyles.

> The greatest quality of excellence is demonstrated by the desire to increase the capacity of the container.

PSALM 33:1–5

This psalm tells us that biblical praise involves musicians who "play skillfully." In other words, praise is not a haphazard exercise.

Sing for joy in the LORD, O you righteous ones;
Praise is becoming to the upright.
Give thanks to the LORD with the lyre;
Sing praises to Him with a harp of ten strings.
Sing to Him a new song;
Play skillfully with a shout of joy.
For the word of the LORD is upright;
And all His work is done in faithfulness.
He loves righteousness and justice;
The earth is full of the lovingkindness of the LORD.

QUALIFICATIONS FOR WORSHIP LEADERS

Because I view the entire worship team as leaders, there are some qualification standards that are important enough to put down on paper. The rules are not that fiercely rigid, just clearly defined for the sake of the whole team and its growth together. The first four are heart issues that require some thought and prayer.

1. Motivation

Motive identification is the first thing I like to find out from all who audition for the worship team. Through a series of questions, I ask each person why he or she wants to participate in worship ministry to this degree. There are no right or wrong answers, but the questions give me a framework from which to challenge each worship team member to another level of understanding. Here are some questions I encourage them to ask themselves:

▲ Why do I do what I do?

▲ Is there something I need to prove to others or to myself?

▲ What do I hope to accomplish by doing this?

▲ Do I feel more accepted by God when I perform this function of ministry?

▲ Is my sense of validity or significance found in this activity?

▲ Must I be seen by others in order to appreciate myself?

▲ Can I allow my individual gift to be a contribution to the whole without fear of being absorbed?

▲ What if I am not chosen as part of the team?

Answering the above questions will help you with the next section.

2. Authority

We have probably all experienced abuses of authority in one form or another through our lives. And as fervently as we may try to escape the confines of this fact, someone in some way will always be our authority. It's best to understand this concept early in life. Who is the leader, and how well can you follow? Where does the proverbial "buck stop"?

With regard to time limits and acceptable forms of worship, who governs—the worship leader or the pastor? What infrastructure of understanding is in place to administrate spontaneous expressions like dance, banners, prophetic acts or the gifts of the Spirit? What is the relationship between the worship leader and the pastor? Are they seen as working together to accomplish a goal, or is there competition to see what can move the people more effectively—the worship or the Word?

One of the greatest challenges in the church today is merging strong personalities in ministry together. In Charismatic or Third-Wave congregations, worship plays a very important role, as does the teaching of the Word. There can be great competition between these two factors, and the result can have potentially damaging spiritual and relationship ramifications.

A note to worship leaders

Discuss the specific guidelines of your position and define the differences of responsibility and authority with your pastor. You are responsible for a task, but what authority do you have to correct a problem within the boundaries of your jurisdiction? Know and understand your role clearly, and communicate your understanding regularly with your leader.

Many pastors have confided to me that they don't know how to relate to their worship leaders. They see them as emotionally unstable, flamboyant one moment and depressed the next. It's as though musicians are searching for something just outside their reach, and when they can't find it, chaos rules, and everyone around them pays dearly. Pastors seldom understand the plight of some creative musicians who live on the edge of reality, having one foot in the natural realm and one in the ozonosphere, waiting for that burst of inspiration to carry their spontaneous creativity into the next service. The administratively sturdy musician is an enigma to the rest of us as we covetously sit and ponder his or her gift mix.

The bottom line is this: Get comfortable with the person God made you to be, and endeavor to change those things that have become bad habits in the areas of preparation, communication and follow through. Do not be ashamed of your humanity, but don't use it as a way to excuse irresponsibility. There are reasons for everything but excuses for nothing. Help your pastor help you!

A note to worship team members

Know who is responsible for setting policies, procedures and rehearsal times within the team. It is vital that you know what your role is and the structure within which you must operate. Submit yourself and your gift to your leader regardless of who may be more talented, educated or gifted. This is a test of humility God delights in proctoring. Remember, "God resists the proud, but gives grace to the humble" (James 4:6, NKJV).

I was in a situation once where I knew that I was more musically inclined, more talented and trained than the leader I was supporting. I was frequently tested in the area of humility! Our methods of leadership differed, and of course, I thought

> ▲ Know and
> ▲ understand your
> ▲ role clearly, and
> ▲ communicate
> ▲ your under-
> ▲ standing regu-
> ▲ larly with your
> ▲ leader.

my way was better. Be that as it may, it took almost three years for the Lord to work the spirit of Absalom out of me. I "submitted" on the exterior, but it seemed my interior was often standing up and shaking a fist! Thank God for His patience.

The Bible teaches a lot about authority and submission. These Scriptures would be of great benefit as an independent study. (Use a concordance for this study.) The Lord's own words will get you started: "Blessed are the meek [humble and teachable]: for they shall inherit the earth" (Matt. 5:5, KJV).

Read Romans 13:1. What did the apostle Paul give as the reason we should submit to those in authority over us?

_____

_____

▲▲▲▲▲▲▲

Read Romans 13:2. What happens if we rebel against God-ordained authority?

_____

_____

▲▲▲▲▲▲▲

Read 1 Timothy 2:1–3. How did Paul recommend we respond toward the various leaders in our lives?

_____

_____

▲▲▲▲▲▲▲

PSALM 150—LET EVERYTHING THAT HATH BREATH

This hymn is based on a psalm that calls for extravagant music. Although some religious people prefer church music to be soft and reverent, we must remember that the Bible often calls for loud and resounding praise!

Praise ye the Lord. Praise God in His sanctuary.
Praise Him in the firmament of His power.
Praise Him on the loud cymbals.
Praise Him on the high sounding cymbals.
Let everything that hath breath praise the Lord. Praise ye the Lord![2]

3. Faithfulness

By definition, *faithfulness* is a commitment or pledge to do something. It is "maintaining allegiance to someone or something; constant, loyal, showing a strong sense of duty or responsibility; conscientious." It implies a continued and steadfast adherence to a person or thing to which one is bound by oath, duty or obligation.

Faithfulness by its mere mention screams *commitment*. For some musicians, commitment is one of the scariest words in the dictionary. It's similar to signing their life away on a mortgage or approving personal organs for donation. It seems so final. But if someone cannot be faithful to a rehearsal, what makes me think that person will be faithful to services or special events? Building a skillful team will require this ingredient of stability.

Faithfulness includes the personal disciplines of prayer and Scripture reading, accountability to a prayer partner or discipler and loyalty to the policies described by the leader's vision. Here's the personal question: Am I able to support the direction of this vision and make it my own?

Read 1 Corinthians 4:1–2. What does God require of those who serve Him?

_____

_____

▲▲▲▲▲▲▲

Read Galatians 5:22–23. Faithfulness is the result of what work in our lives?

_____

_____

▲▲▲▲▲▲▲

4. Holiness

Holiness is the priestly call upon our lives. It is not being called upon by God to *perform* at some perfected level. The Levites were the first to experience being separated unto the Lord. After completing the ceremonial washing and putting on the proper clothing, they were set apart unto God for His service. God told the Hebrews, "You shall be holy, for I am holy" (1 Pet. 1:16). Holiness means being separated *to* God—instead of being separated *from* the world or the ordinary. God's words were more a statement of promise that one day His people could and would be holy because God was. Since He was a holy God, then obviously His people would also be holy, due to His supernatural characteristics.

Unfortunately, Israel did not choose God's holiness as its standard, and the Israelites continued to stray away from God's holy plan. He was faithful through the centuries to send messengers who would instruct them back to His way. But they continually refused prophetic insights and diluted God's purpose.

As members of the New Testament church, holiness is our response to the privilege of knowing God and being called His own—a people for His own possession. (Read Deuteronomy 7:6; 1 Peter 2:9.) Holiness is not a license to act strangely or to treat people differently as a statement of separatism. Holiness is being *separated*, but not *isolated*. If we

> Holiness is the priestly call upon our lives.

must resort to external things alone to prove we are holy, it is possible that a performance mentality is plaguing the inward fiber of character. Such a mentality asserts that God looks upon the outward appearance more than the heart—a false assertion.

The pursuit of holiness begins with the simplicity of accepting what Jesus accomplished on the cross to secure our access to the throne of God—nothing more, nothing less! He created a way for us to be holy through His blood, so let us daily allow it to cleanse and purify our deepest parts.

Read Colossians 1:21–22. Holiness is not something we can accomplish in our own human strength. On what basis are we considered to be holy?

_____

_____

▲▲▲▲▲▲▲

5. Sensitivity to the Spirit

Someone once said, "Success in my life is directly related to my ability to hear and obey the voice of the Holy Spirit." Hearing—and obeying—the voice of the Holy Spirit is a cultivated art—one that is not earned. Listening intently to someone speaking to you gives you an advantage over a person who casually glides into a room and overhears a conversation. The same is true of cultivating sensitivity. Sensitivity takes an investment of time and energy through personal devotion, spiritual focus and what I've heard referred to as "the consistent silent communication with the presence of God."

Sensitivity to the Spirit in a worship service can either "make it" or "break it." To illustrate this point, we must remember that the Holy Spirit is not emotionally unstable! It takes more than a wrong turn or a sour note to grieve or quench Him. Because the Spirit knows the mind of God, and God knows everything, it stands to reason that the Spirit knows the hearts and minds of people before they come into the worship center. If we can sensitize our ears to the Spirit's voice, we also can know the needs of the people and lead them accordingly.

Years ago while leading a worship service, I felt as though we were not hitting the mark. I stood at the keyboard waiting and listening for direction from the Lord. I then realized that I had broken cardinal rule number one: A worship leader must first provide common ground with which everyone can identify. Then he or she must endeavor to move the people together toward their common goal—the throne. I had begun the worship time with a nonuniversal concept, and I foolishly expected the people to follow.

After standing back and reviewing the preceding fifteen minutes of worship, the Holy Spirit spoke to me, telling me to "back up and start again." Humbled by my obvious *faux pas*, I did as I heard Him say. I exhorted the people to reflect on the goodness of God by remembering from where He had brought them. And from there we were able to give thanks for His saving grace and delivering power. As we experienced common ground in our thinking, we were propelled toward unity around the throne.

When the worship times do not "fly," you can simply plow through to the next song and hope for the best, or you can listen to the Spirit who can connect you with better strategies. Allowing you to stand there feeling like an idiot is one of the many ways God proves His ways are better.

Read 1 Corinthians 2:12. The apostle Paul taught that every believer has received the Holy Spirit, who will lead us in the ways of God. What did Paul say the Spirit will reveal to us?

_____

_____

▲▲▲▲▲▲▲

Read Romans 8:26. What does the Holy Spirit do when we rely on and respond to Him?

_____

_____

▲▲▲▲▲▲▲

6. Skill

You may think it strange that "skill" is addressed toward the end of this chapter. But again we must see that true worship musicianship is not about talent and skill alone—it's about heart! Skill is really the icing on the cake for the called musician and an invitation for God to increase the capacity of the container.

I'm constantly encouraging musicians and artistic creators to increase the borders of their territory. Go beyond what you think you can do. There's nothing wrong with studying to perfect your craft. In fact, within our current culture, it is imperative. Paul told Timothy, "Be diligent to present yourself approved to God as a workman who does not need to be ashamed, handling accurately the word of truth" (2 Tim. 2:15). Paul's advice to Timothy was that he should study if he was going to preach the Word. I like the parallel truth here. If we are to lead people into the presence of God, should the requirement be any less?

Kingdom musicians should have a better grasp on chart reading, dynamics, interpretation and spontaneity than non-kingdom musicians. We have the power of the Spirit to energize our hearts and minds to comprehend and communicate through music. Many say they don't have the time or money to invest in lessons. That's understandable, given the busyness of our culture. Still, the choice is up to us. Determine what the call of God is upon your life, and do whatever is possible to build an altar with it. Some things must be sacrificed for the sake of the call. Find out what they are, and offer them to God. What consumes your time that can be given up to increase your craft?

Read 2 Samuel 24:24. King David placed a high value on the types of sacrifices he offered God. What type of offering did he feel was not good enough to give?

_____

_____

_____

▲▲▲▲▲▲▲

With a focused heart, not only can skill increase, but also creativity. Over the past decade, creativity in the form of new music has been on the rise among God's people. More and more musicians are connecting to the purposes of God as they conceptualize God's current word through personal worship. Musicians from around the world are beginning to see the importance of personal creativity before promoting their music via the public media.

WITH ONE VOICE

In recent years, many churches have become more open to celebratory music that involves drums, cymbals, tambourines and other percussion instruments. This is certainly in accord with the biblical model of Davidic worship.

> Break out the cymbals and tambourines,
> Call up the trumpets and horns;
> Raise up a banner and come with me,
> It's time to worship the Lord.
> Praise Him together in unity,
> We've got a reason to sing;
> Lift up a heavenly harmony,
> it's time to worship the King.

▲
▲ Determine what
▲ the call of God
▲ is upon your
▲ life, and do
▲ whatever is pos-
▲ sible to build an
▲ altar with it.
▲

With one voice,
Ev'ry tribe will praise Him
With one voice,
Ev'ry tongue will tell
That the Lord is good;
His love endures
And His mercy lasts forever.

With one voice,
Come and worship,
Lift your voice,
We will worship;
With one voice,
Come and worship
With one voice![3]

One avenue for creativity can be found during private devotional times. As a pianist and vocalist, I like to vary my quiet times with music. Some call it "practicing the presence of God." I look for the best atmosphere to soothe my soul when I come to God. If I can't find it, then I create it with the keyboard or the CD player. Often I'll open the Book of Psalms and begin to interpret them spontaneously on my instrument. And before long, I find my niche with the Lord being carved out right in front of me. I'm able to hear fresh things, melodies, chords and lyrics. Scores of songs have been written like that.

I know of some dancers who do something similar. They'll put on some worship CDs and spontaneously begin to interpret through their craft. Entire musical productions have been choreographed in this fashion, utilizing creativity that abides in the inner being by the Spirit.

The spiritual purpose of skill and creativity is not to make the artist popular or in demand! The purpose is to draw others into the participation of worship. The artist does this by allowing his or her unique gifts to function as a *vehicle* instead of a *focal point*. But the church has been notorious for capitalizing on the most current craze and phenomenon surrounding a "gifted" person or persons. Promotion of gifts alone produces an anemic and dysfunctional minister. Chenaniah, one of King David's appointed chief musician and worship leaders, was in charge of the singing and gave instruction in singing "because he was skillful" (1 Chron. 15:22). His job as a leader was to help others accomplish their task of singing unto the Lord, not to enjoy the icon pedestal.

As was discussed in the last chapter, liturgy is the form by which we offer worship. It is the work of the people in response to God. The worship team is an aid to this end. But too often our worship becomes, and remains, platform driven by the best vocalists and kicking bands available. The concert mentality prevails, allowing the "professionals" to express their hearts through their craft *for* us. We applaud when we think they've done a good job or when it touches us so deeply that we feel better, using spiritual terminology like, "Oh, that was so anointed today…"

Yes, we are to pursue excellence—but for whose benefit? It's for the benefit of the people in their worship to God! Ultimately, God gets the glory! Unfortunately many people have been trained to watch those on the platform and to respond to the band's performance of a great song about God. I've often wondered, *Are they cheering for God or the band? Are these expressions a genuine overflow of the heart of worship or simply a Pavlov's dog facsimile?*

▲▲▲

May the Lord teach us to be shepherds who care for and lead His sheep to places of rest in His presence.

▲▲▲

We are all products of teaching, training and relevant experience. And human nature naturally gravitates toward the worship of idols—even in the church. If we've received inspiration from someone who was a vessel whom the Lord used to bring revelation to us, often our eyes turn to him or her immediately to meet our next need. *If God used that person in the past, surely He will again, right?* I know people who have followed a renowned Bible teacher to countless meetings and conferences for years, waiting for the next nugget of truth.

Did someone teach them to think this way, or was it a natural response? Arguably the latter.

People, like sheep, need to be led. And contrary to what some may say, not all sheep are stupid. They know enough to eat when they're hungry and to run when they're scared. What I'm talking about is the "resting process." Lead the sheep to safety, and they will be peaceful. The psalmist pictured himself as a little sheep who was looking to God, his Shepherd, to care for him when he said, "He makes me lie down in green pastures; He leads me beside quiet waters" (Ps. 23:2).

The difference between a shepherd and a cattle herder is that one leads—the other drives. As we lead God's sheep, may the Lord teach us to be shepherds who care for and lead them to places of rest in His presence.

Leading worship is taking the congregation to a place where they are introduced to God's menu and agenda. He wants both to feed us and to lead us to implement His will.

LET'S TALK ABOUT IT

▲ Why is it important to offer our best when we come together for corporate worship?

_____

_____

▲▲▲▲▲▲▲

▲ How does leading worship with the right motivation enhance the corporate worship experience?

_____

_____

▲▲▲▲▲▲▲

▲ How does leading with the wrong motivation hinder it?

_____

_____

▲▲▲▲▲▲▲

▲ Describe a time when you learned the importance of faithfulness.

_____

_____

▲▲▲▲▲▲▲

▲ What steps can you take to develop more sensitivity to the voice of the Holy Spirit?

_____

_____

▲▲▲▲▲▲▲

YOUR TIME WITH GOD

Father, I don't want my worship of You to be a haphazard experience or a dry routine. I want to offer my whole heart to You. I ask that You correct my motivations and demolish any secret agendas that would hinder my truly being able to commune with You. I offer You the best of my talents, and I ask that You help me to grow in them. I pray that I would be found faithful in Your sight. Teach me to be more sensitive to the leading of the Holy Spirit.

Spiritual Gifts, Intercession and Worship

A TIME OF CONTEMPLATION FOLLOWED A DEEPLY SPIRITUAL TIME OF WORSHIP. Everyone was standing in awe of the presence of God, eyes closed and hands lifted. Suddenly from the furthest region of the room, someone broke the meditative silence, lifted his voice and began speaking what sounded like a prophetic message. It was something about changing perspectives to see things God's way.

Encouraged by the "amens" rippling through the room, the man continued with the exhortation, gaining momentum. He concluded with a point of action—because God looks down from heaven and sees things in a particular way, the people were instructed to climb up on their chairs and look down on the floor. After that they were told to jump back down to the floor, march seven times around their chairs, shout "Hallelujah" and watch God do a miracle. They did— and were embarrassingly ashamed to admit they had no idea what they were doing or why.

The first part of the prophetic exhortation was good. We all need an occasional perspective change. But the action part got a little scary. Now, I agree with the apostle Paul's directive: "Despise not prophesyings" (1 Thess. 5:20, KJV). But it's dangerous to believe every word without it being tested by Scripture and by the prophets in the house. Things could get lethal if we do not test prophetic words by the wisdom of God while giving direction to His flock. In this case, "poor spiritual stewardship" could have been one of the railing accusations against local leadership.

This is a simple illustration of how goofy things can get in a moment of prophetic passion without proper discernment.

After worshiping for forty-five minutes, these hungry people were aware of the Holy Spirit's hovering as they waited on the Lord for His voice of comfort, approval or instruction. What they got was a unique display of strangeness beneath the guise of "freedom in the Spirit." The flow of what the Holy Spirit was doing in the congregation that morning was truly deep. But the abrupt change of direction in activity brought some confusion.

Perhaps you've experienced things like this. In some locations, the stranger things are, the more spiritual they are interpreted to be. Yet many are still wandering around looking for answers to the weirdness that has characterized their religious encounters. Now they are leery of anything related to a "spiritual experience."

Of course, God is not the author of such confusion (1 Cor. 14:33). He would rather us be informed about Him and His ways in order to avoid the misuses of Scripture and experiences that some people would put on us. For many of these people, their experience is real. However, when they begin to superimpose their spiritual encounter on others, shame can occur.

> For God is not a God of confusion but of peace.
> —1 Corinthians 14:33

▲▲

Our worship creates a platform or an atmosphere in which the Holy Spirit can minister to the hearts of men and women, convict them of sin and change the direction of their lives.

▲▲

Two things are certain—heaven is speaking, and the gifts of the Spirit are in operation today. Whoever has an ear can hear what the Spirit is saying to His church. (Read Revelation 3:6.) When John baptized Jesus in the Jordan River, the Bible says that God spoke from heaven. Some thought it had only thundered. Whatever manner God chooses to speak through, let our interest be kindled and our ears tuned.

When we posture our hearts in worship before the presence of almighty God, He is then able to speak to us. Our worship creates a platform or an atmosphere in which the Holy Spirit can minister to the hearts of men and women, convict them of sin and change the direction of their lives.

There are a number of ways He can do this. The voice of God is often heard in the congregation through the administration of the gifts of the Spirit. At a particular point in a moment of reflection after our offerings of worship have been presented, someone may offer an unknown tongue and an interpretation, a word of prophecy or an exhortation by the Spirit to include a word of knowledge or word of wisdom.

Sometimes, as was discussed in chapter five, the song of the Lord will be sung by an individual, which can lead to a congregational response of spontaneous nature. Perhaps a message *from* God is sung to the congregation by a soloist or the congregation sings a message *to* God. In either case, depending on if it is sung in a known tongue (in the understanding) or an unknown tongue (in the spirit), this is primarily a manifestation of the gift of prophecy using music and song as the vehicle.

> Worship leads us into a place of supernatural power.

Read 1 Corinthians 14:1, 39. What did the apostle Paul say our attitude should be regarding spiritual gifts?

_____

_____

▲▲▲▲▲▲▲

Read 1 Corinthians 14:3. Why is the gift of prophecy so important?

_____

_____

▲▲▲▲▲▲▲

Read 1 John 4:1. What did the apostle John say we were to do with prophetic words before receiving and acting upon them?

_____

_____

▲▲▲▲▲▲▲

When hearts are open to receive, I usually conclude that our worship time has been successful or has "hit the mark." When Jesus is glorified and has connected with His people, I call that "mission accomplished"! The power of God can then rearrange our philosophy of life by infusing us with His ideals. Though the Holy Spirit may utilize the gifts of the Spirit, God can speak to us quietly, personally and just as effectively in the depths of our being with the power of His *still, small voice* (1 Kings 19:13).

In Paul's first letter to the Corinthians, he addresses several issues of concern in the church. He covers topics like foundations for life, immorality, marriage, business, the Lord's Table and spiritual gifts. Then in chapter 14 he gives a prescription for releasing the gifts in a congregational setting. He lays it out in a fashion that is nonthreatening and user-friendly.

Remaining aware that the gifts of the Spirit are for edification, exhortation, comfort and correction, we indeed want to hear what the Spirit of God needs to say to our local churches. Reading through 1 Corinthians 14, you can see the clarity Paul brings to the procedure for releasing and using the gifts. His closing remarks state, "But everything should be done in a fitting and orderly way" (1 Cor. 14:40, NIV). Every local church leadership team has its respective methods for discerning and releasing the vocal gifts during services.

Worship leads us into a place of supernatural power and welcomes the Holy Spirit to move among His people. At times the Spirit will impress upon someone that a gift of healing or miracles is present. Instruction may be given for those in need to come forward and receive something supernatural from God. The Bible teaches us that God performs signs, wonders and miracles for several reasons (Exod. 9:14–16):

▲ To prove there is none like Him in all the earth
▲ So His glory can be revealed
▲ For His name to be proclaimed
▲ For the fear of the Lord to fall upon people

The Holy Spirit releases His gifts to be used to minister to the needs of people, but His first objective is to draw attention to God's majestic greatness! He wants everyone to recognize the awesomeness of God as He releases faith for miracles.

And behold, a voice came to him and said, "What are you doing here, Elijah?"
—1 Kings 19:13

I will send all My plagues...so that you may know that there is no one like Me in all the earth. For if by now I had put forth My hand and struck you...with pestilence, you would then have been cut off from the earth. But, indeed, for this cause I have allowed you to remain, in order to show you My power, and in order to proclaim My name through all the earth.
—Exodus 9:14–16

PSALM 67:1–7

This psalm reminds us that as God's presence dwells with His people, the natural result will be an impact on the surrounding society.

> God be gracious to us and bless us,
> And cause His face to shine upon us—Selah.
> That Thy way may be known on the earth,
> Thy salvation among all nations.
> Let the peoples praise Thee, O God;
> Let all the peoples praise Thee.
> Let the nations be glad and sing for joy;
> For Thou wilt judge the peoples with uprightness,
> And guide the nations on the earth. Selah.
> Let the peoples praise Thee, O God;
> Let all the peoples praise Thee.
> The earth has yielded its produce;
> God, our God, blesses us.
> God blesses us,
> That all the ends of the earth may fear Him.

WORSHIP AND THE REALM OF THE ETERNAL

Eternity, where God lives, is outside of space and time. When our hearts are joined with His, heaven and earth meet. Eternal purpose is facilitated and realized. When we worship, we are joining the hosts of heaven and the great "cloud of witnesses"—the saints who have gone before us (Heb. 12:1).

The writer of Hebrews makes a fascinating point about the joining of heaven and earth in worship:

> *But you have come to Mount Zion and to the city of the living God, the heavenly Jerusalem, and to myriads of angels, to the general assembly and church of the first-born who are enrolled in heaven, and to God, the Judge of all, and to the spirits of righteous men made perfect, and to Jesus, the mediator of a new covenant...*
>
> —HEBREWS 12:22–24

Through a merging of ideas here, we discover that there is

no distinction between the worshiping church on the earth and the heavenly Jerusalem, or the city of God. This reinforces Jesus' statement that the true worshiper will worship the Father in Spirit and truth. No longer is God bound to any kind of earthly temple in which to be worshiped. But by the Spirit He has created a superhighway between the heavenly and earthly spheres for the sake of joining the natural and supernatural elements of worship.

The following ancient prayer and creed of the church, rich in doctrinal truth and heritage, provides a sense of unity with ages past and will continue to serve that purpose long after we are gone. Notice the words regarding the church in heaven and on earth.

Te Deum Laudemus

We praise Thee, O God, we acknowledge Thee to
    be Lord.
All the earth doth worship Thee, the Father everlasting.
To Thee all angels cry aloud, the heavens and all the
    powers therein;
To Thee the cherubim and seraphim do continually cry,
Holy, holy, holy, Lord God of Sabaoth:
Heaven and earth are full of the majesty of Thy glory.
The glorious company of the apostles praise Thee.
The goodly fellowship of the prophets praise Thee.
The noble army of the martyrs praise Thee.
The holy Church throughout all the world doth
    acknowledge Thee.
The Father of infinite majesty;
Thine adorable, true and only Son;
Also the Holy Ghost, the Comforter.[1]

HEAVEN'S MODEL OF WORSHIP

Heaven existed before earth, thus the example of heaven's worship supersedes that of earth. Heaven is perfectly complete, and its model provides the perfect prototype for genuine worship. (Read Hebrews 9:23.) The Old Covenant tabernacle was a small-scale replica of what is found in

For it was fitting for Him, for whom are all things, and through whom are all things, in bringing many sons to glory, to perfect the author of their salvation through sufferings.

—Hebrews 2:10

heaven, but in heaven, the throne of God replaces the ark of the covenant. The throne is God's "chair." It is not the place where He kicks back to rest or relax—that would be the mercy seat where the blood of Jesus has satisfied God's righteous and holy requirement for sin. His throne, however, is the place and position from which He rules heaven, earth and the consummate universe.

When God received the blood of Jesus upon the mercy seat as the ultimate sacrifice for sin, He rested from His labor in creation and redemption. His reward was the many souls who have been brought to glory through Christ's sacrifice (Heb. 2:10). Now the true owner and sovereign of the cosmos has been reinstated to righteous rule by His death on a wooden cross.

> Suspended between heaven and earth, Jesus said, "It is finished!" For all practical purposes, Jesus may as well have said, "The purchase is complete. I now present the earth and its fullness back to You, Father!" The most incredible event in history has been recorded in the annals of heaven, bringing the worship of the Creator into another dimension with a new title, "Redeemer." Now sitting on the throne, He exercises His governmental role as Ruler of all. Jesus is the focus and "object" of our worship as He is the One who made it possible for us to minister before the throne of God. [2]

Read Psalm 99:5. Why did the psalmist say we should worship God at His footstool?

_____

_____

▲▲▲▲▲▲▲

Read Hebrews 4:16. How did the apostle Paul describe God's throne?

_____

_____

▲▲▲▲▲▲▲

What impact does knowing that have on our lives?

_____

_____

▲▲▲▲▲▲▲

Heaven is *eternal*—meaning it has no end. The concept of eternity mystifies us because there's no way to truly describe or appreciate "forever"—unless, of course, you're waiting for your wife to finish shopping or you're stuck in a downtown Dallas freeway traffic jam. Even then, you'll probably get home for dinner, albeit two or more hours late.

To think that the worship of God will go on for eternity is mind boggling. Will we get tired or run out of things to say and sing? As humans perceiving things from a natural world, that would be the case. But not in heaven! I once heard someone describe the cherubim and seraphim in heaven. They cover their eyes with their wings. When they uncover them and look upon the Lamb, they see a brand-new facet of His glorious being revealed, to which they erupt with a passionate, invigorating "Holy, holy, holy!" And this goes on *forever*… and ever…!

The eternal nature of worship is what makes this aspect of the church's ministry so vital. Worship is one occupation that will last forever! As valid as many Christian activities are, they are but a temporary overflow of the life we have in Jesus that's meant to be shared with the world. An instructor of missiology, and a strong supporter of the Great Commission, Pastor John Piper writes:

> **Worship is one occupation that will last forever.**

> Missions is not the ultimate goal of the church. Worship is. Missions exists because worship doesn't. Worship is ultimate, not missions, because God is ultimate, not man. When this age is over, and the countless millions of the redeemed fall on their faces before the throne of God, missions will be no more. It is a temporary necessity. But worship abides forever.[3]

This is an incredibly powerful concept that is often missed by the church. We've viewed worship as a means to an end, rather than as the focus of our eternal beings. We sometimes feel a need to "get on with kingdom business" after we've worshiped, as if worship were a warm-up to something greater yet ahead. This erroneous stream of thought is completely contrary to Scripture. Because the worship of God will last forever, everything we do in this life is a precursor to the eternal finale of endless waves of worship around the throne, offered by people from every nation, tribe and tongue.

First Corinthians 13 informs us that gifts of prophecy, tongues and words of knowledge will cease when the perfect comes, as these are but a means to an end. The bottom line is *agape love*. This love of God and the worship of God, who is love, abide forever in the domain of eternity and far surpass our ability to either understand or explain.

Worship also elevates us into a realm of rulership where we are seated with Christ in heavenly places (Eph. 2:6). The Scriptures also teach that since the church is seated with Christ in the heavenly realms, we are to make "the manifold wisdom of God... known... to the rulers and the authorities in the heavenly places" (Eph. 3:10). We have a responsibility as the church of the living God to inform principalities and powers that they no longer have authority. (This will be discussed more thoroughly in the next chapter.)

> ...and raised us up with Him, and seated us with Him in the heavenly places, in Christ Jesus.
>
> —Ephesians 2:6

GOD OF GRACE AND GOD OF GLORY

Harry Emerson Fosdick (1878–1969) preached in the early part of the twentieth century at First Presbyterian Church of the City of New York. He struggled deeply over the divisions that were emerging between "liberal" and "conservative" Christians.

God of grace and God of glory,
On Thy people pour Thy power;
Crown Thine ancient church's story,
Bring her bud to glorious flower.
Grant us wisdom, grant us courage,
For the facing of this hour,
For the facing of this hour.

Lo! The hosts of evil round us
Scorn Thy Christ, assail Thy ways!
Fears and doubts too long have bound us,
Free our hearts to faith and praise.

Grant us wisdom, grant us courage,
For the living of these days,
For the living of these days.[4]

INTERCESSION AND WORSHIP

There's really nothing more important in our relationship with God than worship and prayer. The two are matched as lifelines to the presence of God. As clear as this is becoming to the body of Christ, still there are some who see worship and prayer as separate functions. Worship is for singing with music; prayer is for speaking out petitions. But can the two be combined?

▲▲▲

Worship and prayer become the convergence
of God's heart and His agenda—
His pleasure and purpose.

▲▲▲

Yes! In the midst of giving pleasure to God in worship, He can accomplish His purpose by transforming our minds, giving us His heart for others. Worship and prayer become the convergence of God's heart and His agenda—His pleasure and purpose.

When the disciples asked Jesus to teach them to pray, Jesus responded with a prayer format that we call "The Lord's Prayer." This prayer is basically outlined as a combination of worship and prayer. The first part is worship to God; the second is prayer for our needs. Jesus starts with, "Our Father who art in heaven, hallowed be Thy name" (Matt. 6:9). He was saying that we should begin prayer by worshiping the name of the Lord. To *hallow* is to reverence, sanctify as holy or show deep respect.

Jesus continues with, "Thy kingdom come. Thy will be done…" (v. 10). Worship continues as God's kingly rule is exalted. Jesus teaches that we should ask for God's sovereign administration and authority to come here on earth.

After worship has been established and the focus of our hearts is turned toward God's almighty power, the vertical direction then changes to horizontal as Jesus instructs us to ask for God to meet our personal needs: "Give us this day our daily bread" (v. 11). In simpler terms, He said we should ask God to provide for us. Then, "Forgive us our debts, as we also have forgiven our debtors" (v. 12). This clearly reveals our need to be cleansed and forgiven, but only as we forgive others. The final petition is, "And do not lead us into temptation, but deliver us from [the] evil [one]" (v. 13). This is a genuine cry to be kept from the evil traps of the enemy.

Looking intently at this form, Jesus was not prescribing this prayer to be recited—He was describing the ingredients for communion with God. Worship and prayer are hand-in-hand components in a healthy relationship for every believer.

Although we are discussing the merging of worship and prayer, the most important thing I'd like to point out about the model prayer is that worship precedes petition. Before we launch headlong into asking things of God, He must be placed in the highest position.

There is much to be said about the simultaneous offerings of prayer and worship. Dietrich Bonhoeffer, a contemporary martyr of the faith, wrote about what is truly important:

> … not what we want to pray… but what God wants us to pray. If we were dependent entirely on ourselves, we would probably pray only the fourth petition of the Lord's Prayer [*deliver us from the evil one*]. But God wants it otherwise. The richness of the Word of God ought to determine our prayer, not the poverty of our heart.[5]

If we allow the poverty of our hearts to dictate our prayers and worship, we run the risk of diminishing once again the purpose of corporate worship to meeting our individual needs. But if we worship in the way He initiates, our needs will be met as a residual effect of obeying God. According to Jesus, if we seek His kingdom and His right-eousness first, then all our personal needs will be met (Matt. 6:33).

But seek first His kingdom and His righteousness; and all these things shall be added to you.

—Matthew 6:33

Read Psalm 149:3–4. When we worship the Lord, what does it bring Him?

_____

_____

▲▲▲▲▲▲▲

Read 1 Timothy 2:1–4. Why is intercession such an important aspect of our worship?

_____

_____

▲▲▲▲▲▲▲

Read Hebrews 7:25. Who is our partner in intercession?

_____

_____

▲▲▲▲▲▲▲

The prophet Isaiah depicted the marriage of prayer and praise as he spoke for God in the following passage: "My house will be called a house of prayer for all the peoples" (Isa. 56:7). The words *of prayer* (*tephillah* in Hebrew) communicate a prayer that is set to music and sung in formal worship. Literally, *tephillah* means "an intercessory song"; it appears seventy-seven times in the Old Testament. In other words… "My house will be called a house of prayer and praise."

From the beginning, the heart of God's covenant has been toward the nations of the earth. As Creator of all it would be incongruous for Him to relinquish His right to all the nations but Israel. "The earth is the LORD's, and all it contains" (Ps. 24:1). It is evident that all things belong to Him and that He intends to keep it that way. The nations of the earth are God's possession, and, as a joint inheritance, His family has been commissioned to secure them with Jesus.

God's desire to give the nations as an inheritance to Jesus can be heard in the words of an obscure Old Testament prophet:

"In that day I will raise up the fallen booth [tabernacle] of David, and wall up its breaches; I will also raise up its ruins, and rebuild it as in the days of old; that they may possess the remnant of Edom and all the nations [or Gentiles] who are called by My name," declares the LORD who does this.
—AMOS 9:11–12

As we discussed in an earlier chapter, the tabernacle of David was the Old Covenant epitome of free access to the holy place. Intimate fellowship with God was experienced through spontaneous worship, then manifestations of His presence would follow. God's purpose in restoring David's tabernacle was for the nations to be welcomed into His covenant. God wanted to show Himself to all the peoples, using Israel as a prototype of true covenantal relationship.

The tabernacle of David can be seen as a commissioning center for God's people to possess the nations. God's promise to restore both the worship of His name and His people's inheritance comes through crystal clear. This "restoration" of the tabernacle began when Jesus the Messiah was born, and His ministry of reconciliation for all people groups continues today through His covenant believers.

One way in which this tabernacle is rebuilt today is through regular gatherings of worship. As in David's day, there is freedom to minister to the Lord and hear His voice for the things on His heart. This is where some of our "chores" fit into the service of the sanctuary.

So what is the purpose of the "Father's House"? Think about the average family life:

Ideally, the many facets and functions of the family are the spawn of their relationship with one another. Initiated by the head of the household, the chores each one assumes are for the benefit and comfort of the entire family. For example, as a father, I try to keep the household chores interesting and exciting by building into my children an appreciation for one another. I let them know that the personal chores assigned are meant to bless each other—not wreck their lives. Like most of us, sometimes they moan and complain, hoping that someone will take pity on them and excuse them from their drudgery. If I excuse them, however, they won't learn the value of simple disciplines that will definitely bless their future lives.

Keeping the analogy in mind, God's house is designed to function similarly. There are a number of "chores" that must be performed to maintain the health of His family. When we understand these chores and the effect our part plays in the overall scheme of things, we can approach our responsibilities with a sense of valuable participation regardless of whether or not it "feels good" to us. Following Father's agenda for the house will keep us from tailoring our own and wanting to put His name on it.[6]

For the sake of continuity, let's use David's tabernacle as a model for God's house. Combining the concept of the tabernacle with Isaiah's prophecy, the purpose of God's house was to be a house of prayer and praise for all nations, marrying passion for God with His purpose for the earth. There is nothing random about kingdom principles. Everything God does is purpose driven.

Read Psalm 22:27. What did David prophesy all the nations of the earth would do?

_____

_____

▲▲▲▲▲▲▲

Read Philippians 2:4. Worship is not a selfish thing. What principle should be kept in mind as we enter into times of corporate worship?

_____

_____

▲▲▲▲▲▲▲

As was noted earlier, to know God in the deepest sense of the Hebrew word *yadah* is "to have intimate knowledge of Him, similar to the intimacy shared by a husband and wife in marriage." The union pictured in this word is entwining enough for conception to occur. Daniel used this word when he spoke about God's people knowing Him and taking action. "… but the people who *know* their God will display strength and take action" (Dan. 11:32, emphasis added). Though this scripture has been used to support scores of noble—and even militant—Christian activities, this entire passage is in reference to preserving the temple and the true worship of God. Daniel said that those who are intimate with God will be strengthened and zealous enough to take action in maintaining the integrity

> ▲ Oh, that God
> ▲ would find us
> ▲ with such
> ▲ insatiable
> ▲ passion and
> ▲ reverence for
> ▲ Him and His
> ▲ house that in
> ▲ the midst of
> ▲ our worship
> ▲ we might
> ▲ recognize our
> ▲ responsibilities
> ▲ and be
> ▲ empowered to
> ▲ take action in
> ▲ prayer for the
> ▲ nations of
> ▲ the earth.

of His purpose in His house. This sounds rather serious!

The result of this zeal for God's house is the same that Jesus exhibited in Matthew 21:13. Driving out the money-changers, He said to them, "It is written, 'My house shall be called a house of prayer'; but you a making it a robbers' den." God's intention was that His house would be "a house of prayer for all nations" (Isa. 56:7, NIV). But the original divine purpose had been lost, similarly to the prophet Daniel's day.

Today, some people treat the Lord with a random and familiar style that brings Him down to their level so they can feel comfortable. Many of these people still view the house of God as being designed so their own desires can be stroked. They diminish its purpose to satisfy their own gains. Do we come into His house to give, or do we come to take what we can, turning the house of God into a den of thieves? Oh, that God would find us with such insatiable passion and reverence for Him and His house that in the midst of our worship we might recognize our responsibilities and be empowered to take action in prayer for the nations of the earth.

Read 1 Timothy 3:15. Why is the house of God so important?

_____

_____

▲▲▲▲▲▲▲

Read Psalm 26:8. What was David's attitude about the house of God?

_____

_____

▲▲▲▲▲▲▲

SALVATION SPRING UP FROM THE GROUND

This contemporary chorus by Charlie Hall releases a corporate cry to God for a world-wide spiritual awakening. Songs like this one can have a powerful impact in the spiritual realm when we gather for corporate praise, worship and prayer.

Salvation, spring up from the ground;
Lord, rend the heavens and come down.
Seek the lost and heal the lame,
Jesus, bring glory to Your name.

Let all the prodigals run home,
All of creation waits and groans.
Lord, we've heard of Your great fame
Father, cause all to shout Your name.

Stir up our hearts, O God,
Open our spirits to awe who You are;
Put a cry in us so deep inside
That we cannot find the words we need.
We just weep and cry out to You.[7]

Mingled with our "Hallelujahs" and praises to God, we lift up cries of "Hosanna," "Have mercy, Lord. Save NOW!" (Ps. 118:25). The psalmist shows that in the midst of festive celebration and sacrifice, there is a cry from God's people for compassion and deliverance. We worship not only to exalt the name of God, but to implore His saving grace in circumstances needing supernatural intervention.

As we lift up the name of the Lord in worship, it is not only proper but also a necessity to offer prayers and petitions for the nations of the earth. Sensitivity to the leading of the Spirit will reveal how we should intercede for the things on God's heart. By the Spirit we can hear what is pressing on God's agenda for that moment. Perhaps there's a particular ethnic group ready for harvest, and we need to pray for the commissioning of laborers. Or possibly a civil war is about to erupt in some remote area of the world, which could inhibit the progress of the gospel. Whatever the case, it's possible to access God's agenda through the reverence of His name in worship.

Still another passage of Scripture that points to the dual purpose of the worshiper and intercessor is found in the Book of Revelation.

And when He had taken the book, the four living creatures and the twenty-four elders fell down before the Lamb, having each

> O LORD, do save, we beseech Thee; O LORD, we beseech Thee, do send prosperity!
> —Psalm 118:25

*one a harp, and golden bowls full of incense, which are the
prayers of the saints.*

—REVELATION 5:8

The elders in heaven have in their possession a harp and a
bowl. The harp represents worship, and the golden bowl of
incense represents the prayers and intercessions of God's people on the earth. With those items in hand, they sang a new
song, "Worthy art Thou to take the book, and to break its
seals" (v. 9). From a position of worship and prayer, they
acknowledge the Lamb's worth to answer their prayers.

The picture here is that of the Old Testament Levitical
priests offering incense upon the altar. Every time a priest
entered the holy place to trim the wicks on the lampstand or
to set the table of shewbread, he was instructed to sprinkle a
handful of incense upon the altar. The cloud of smoke would
travel through the veil into the holy of holies—into the presence of God. In Revelation, John called this incense "the
prayers of the saints."

> The fragrance was compounded according to a formula given
> to Moses by God in the mount. Four principal spices were
> blended together, signifying that neither prayer nor worship is
> a simple action—both are complex and their components are
> blended according to a divine prescription.[8]

In Revelation 5, John begins to weep for there is no one
worthy to take the book and open its seals. "And one of the
elders said to me, 'Stop weeping; behold, the Lion that is
from the tribe of Judah, the Root of David, has overcome so
as to open the book and its seven seals'" (Rev. 5:5).

▲▲

As we worship and intercede for people and nations, we become God's vehicle and channel in the earth, standing in the gap, releasing Him to act.

▲▲▲▲▲▲▲▲▲▲▲▲▲▲▲▲▲▲▲▲▲▲▲▲▲▲▲▲▲▲▲▲▲▲▲▲▲▲

This is the book of judgments that are released in the sixth
chapter of Revelation. But they are not poured out upon the
earth until after the elders worship with the harp and bowl,

singing the new song, "Worthy art Thou to take the book and to break its seals" (v. 9). And another song is raised, "To Him who sits on the throne, and to the Lamb, be blessing and honor and glory and dominion forever and ever" (v. 13). (According to this scripture, worship releases warfare and judgment. The offensive nature of worship through warfare will be addressed in the next chapter.)

As we worship and intercede for people and nations, we become God's vehicle and channel in the earth, standing in the gap, releasing Him to act. The elders in heaven await our cooperation before handing the vials of prayers to angelic messengers for delivery of the judgments of God. Since God is looking for a people to *pray* His will, our doing so, combined with thanksgiving, releases Him to *do* His will.

Songs of praise and worship in the sanctuary prepare the way for further acts of the Spirit. As we've seen, various "chores of the church" in worship are conducive to the growth of the body and should be viewed as opportunities for joyful, zealous service. Intercession through worship is but another method of maturing a fellowship to look outside their personal arena into the eternal realm where God lives. The way He sees things is a liberating breath of fresh air in our often stale mode of personal need. When the Spirit moves us to intercession in worship, it is such an awesome privilege to be used of God to affect the destinies of men and nations through our worship.

The point of this kind of intercessory worship is for us to bring the "remnants of the peoples" of the earth before the throne of God. This is the ultimate resting place of every redeemed nation, tribe, kindred and tongue—as the scripture says: "All the earth will worship Thee, and will sing praises to Thee" (Ps. 66:4). With eternity in mind, this is true prophetic preparation for the climactic destiny of global worship in heaven.

LET'S TALK ABOUT IT

▲ In the sample prayer Jesus gave His disciples when He taught them how to pray, the first thing He did was exalt God the Father. What can we learn from this in our own times of worship?

_____

_____

▲▲▲▲▲▲▲

▲ Why is it important to seek God first—not the fulfillment of our own needs—when we come together to worship?

_____

_____

▲▲▲▲▲▲▲

▲ What role does worship play in the release of the gifts of the Spirit?

_____

_____

▲▲▲▲▲▲▲

▲ Describe some areas for which you believe God wants you to intercede.

_____

_____

▲▲▲▲▲▲▲

YOUR TIME WITH GOD

Father, my desire is to capture Your heart when I worship. Help me to take my focus off my own needs and desires and to keep my eyes on You. Help my ears to be sensitive to what You are saying. I want to be more available to You so that the Holy Spirit can flow through me to minister to others in the body of Christ. Give me a heart of intercession for those who are lost and those whom You love.

CHAPTER NINE

Worship and Warfare— Scattering His Enemies

THE JOURNEY OF FAITH

T HREE ARMIES WERE ON THEIR WAY. Destruction was imminent! It was a grim reality to an otherwise good day. After all, the kingdom was in order, the people were happy, and there hadn't been drought or war for several years. Everything was going smoothly in the land of Judah. Then King Jehoshaphat received word from his scouts that the armies of Moab, Ammon and Mount Seir had rallied together just beyond the sea. As the scout reported the news to his commander, the enemy forces were en route to invade Judah and take Jerusalem.

Jehoshaphat knew that he had stationed soldiers in all the fortified cities. In addition, there were over a million men in the surrounding territories whom he considered valiant warriors who could fight on his behalf. Still, with the numbers coming up from the lands of Moab, Ammon and Seir, Jehoshaphat's group was no match for the impending swarm of evil soon to arrive.

In absolute terror, Jehoshaphat turned his attention to inquire of the Lord. Knowing it would take a few days for the armies to arrive, he proclaimed a fast throughout the kingdom and gathered the people to Jerusalem to seek the Lord's mercy.

As the king stood in the house of the Lord before the new court, he lifted up his voice and cried out to God. He began by extolling the Lord as the God of the heavens and the ruler of kingdoms and nations. He then spoke of all the Lord had done in the past to secure His people in their land, going back as far as Abraham. He mentioned that they had built the temple and how they had turned to God in times of evil, pestilence, sword and judgment, knowing God would hear their distress and deliver them. He briefed God on the history of these nations coming against the kingdom of Judah.

IN THIS CHAPTER YOU WILL DISCOVER THAT...

▲ Jesus Christ is Lord regardless of what we see with our natural eyes.

▲ As a prophetic people, we function as a vehicle for the verdicts of God to be rendered against spiritual wickedness.

▲ There is nothing more threatening to the powers of darkness than for a group of believers to declare the lordship of Jesus over the entire earth.

Apparently these were three different tribes whose territory Israel was not allowed to invade when they came from Egypt centuries prior. "See how they are repaying us by coming to drive us out of the possession you gave us as an inheritance. O our God, will you not judge them? For we have no power to face this vast army that is attacking us. We do not know what to do, but our eyes are upon you" (2 Chron. 20:11–12, NIV).

After the godly king laid it all out before the Lord without pretense, the Spirit of the Lord came upon Jehaziel in the midst of the congregation, and he prophesied.

> *Do not be afraid or discouraged because of this vast army. For the battle is not yours, but God's. Tomorrow march down against them. They will be climbing up by the Pass of Ziz, and you will find them at the end of the gorge in the Desert of Jeruel. You will not have to fight this battle. Take up your positions; stand firm and see the deliverance the LORD will give you, O Judah and Jerusalem. Do not be afraid; do not be discouraged. Go out to face them tomorrow, and the LORD will be with you.*
> —2 CHRONICLES 20:15–17

Elated by the word of the Lord through Jehaziel, Jehoshaphat and all the people fell down in worship while the Levites stood and praised God with a loud voice.

Early the next morning, the king took his army and went down to the wilderness of Tekoa. Jehoshaphat gave a quick pep talk about trusting in the Lord and His prophets, and then he conferred with the people. The general consensus was to take the Lord at His word and trust what the prophet had said in God's name. Not only that, but they also put a twist on the "trust" part by appointing the singers to go out before the army to praise the Lord. The choir had no time to practice that day. Duty called!

So off they went, singing and praising the Lord, saying, "Give thanks to the LORD, for his love endures forever" (v. 21, NIV). Then the most bizarre thing happened. As worship ascended, the Lord set ambushments against the enemy and destroyed them. The victory was so incredibly overwhelming, the enemy forces then turned on themselves and destroyed one another. When the mayhem ceased, there was so much spoil it took Judah three days to clean up.

What a powerful display of faith and trust! Up to this point in history, there was no precedent for this kind of warfare. It's as if the idea just popped into Jehoshaphat's head overnight. But God honored it as a symbol of faith in Him, and He used the worship of His name to defeat the forces that were opposing His people. What really happened that day as the choir sang the ancient acclamation, "Give thanks to the LORD, for His love endures forever"?

Allow me to reiterate the Old Testament directive. "Give thanks to the LORD," found throughout Scripture, means much more than simply, "Offer praise to God"! The Hebrew word *hodah* meant that to give thanks was to confess Yahweh as King and God. They were recognizing the Lord God as the Supreme One by giving thanks. And in doing so, they covenanted again to honor Him as the only true and living God who would deliver them from their enemies. They were saying, "There is no other God in all the earth… ours is as good as it gets!"

Read Deuteronomy 20:2–4. Why can we be confident in the spiritual battles and challenges we face?

_____

_____

▲▲▲▲▲▲▲

Read 2 Kings 6:16–17. What did God cause the prophet Elisha to see when Israel was confronted by the enemy's army?

_____

_____

▲▲▲▲▲▲▲

Read 1 Chronicles 29:11. Who did King David say is both the focus and the basis of our victory?

_____

_____

▲▲▲▲▲▲▲

PSALM 149:1–9

This psalm makes it clear that when God's people engage in the activity of heaven, the effect can be felt in the demonic realm. Demonic "kings" and the "nobles" of hell can be chained through the power of anointed praise and prayer.

Praise the Lord!
Sing to the Lord a new song,
And His praise in the congregation of the godly ones.

Let Israel be glad in his Maker;
Let the sons of Zion rejoice in their King.
Let them praise His name with dancing;
Let them sing praises to Him with timbrel and lyre.
For the Lord takes pleasure in His people;
He will beautify the afflicted ones with salvation.

Let the godly ones exult in glory;
Let them sing for joy on their beds.
Let the high praises of God be in their mouth,
And a two-edged sword in their hand,
To execute vengeance on the nations,
And punishment on the peoples;
To bind their kings with chains,
And their nobles with fetters of iron;
To execute on them the judgment written;
This is an honor for all His godly ones.
Praise the Lord!

UNDERSTANDING SPIRITUAL WARFARE

There has been a growing awareness of spiritual warfare in the past decade. Written material by qualified teachers and conferences on the subject are increasingly available around the globe. Many have asked about the correlation between worship and warfare, as both seem to be at opposite ends of the spiritual spectrum. There is a fascination with the link that draws us into a deeper awareness of this concept through Scripture.

I've been in worship meetings where someone began the service by welcoming the presence of the Lord in prayer. After giving honor to God for a brief moment, with the next breath the leader began binding principalities and powers, demons of all sorts—even Satan himself—from hindering the meeting. This would go on for a while as the person thought of more things to cast down. By the time the prayer was finished, the people in the congregation had either been taken aback or were worked up into a frenzy, shouting curses at the enemy and pulling down every kind of stronghold imaginable.

Certainly God has called us His army. The analogy of combat definitely includes a good side, a bad side and strategies of warfare. There are casualties that need attention and training schools to better equip soldiers in battle tactics. However, there is an inordinate amount of unhealthy focus on the devil and his demons these days. It seems there is competition between Satan and Jesus like never before. Leaders on every side are warning us about the warfare they are experiencing and instructing us to shore up our reserves to fight.

It is as if God's authority and sovereignty is in question, and we, His people, are going to defend Him against the cruelty of the world and the devil. We've all but believed that it is up to *us* to save every soul, heal every wound and bind every demonic spirit from hindering the work of God in the earth. We think, *If it weren't for us...*

Sometimes God is treated like the god Baal in the story of Elijah and the prophets on Mount Carmel. Four hundred fifty prophets of Baal had gathered with Elijah to determine who the real God was. Elijah said, "The God who answers by fire, He is God" (1 Kings 18:24). That sounded good to the others. Then the show started. From morning until sundown, the prophets of Baal screamed, shouted and cut themselves to get the attention of their god. No reply.

Satan-focused screaming and shouting has been used for years. Those who do it are sometimes viewed as more in tune with the Spirit, discerning, prophetic and the like. Be that as it may, before we quickly lose sight of everything we've already learned, let us remember that Jesus Christ is Lord regardless of what we see with our natural eyes. He rules and reigns over all things in might and power. There's nothing that escapes His attention, because there's nothing He does not know. Rest assured—He's MUCH bigger than the devil. It's preposterous to think there is ANY competition 'twixt the two!

That does not excuse us from remaining alert. We are not ignorant of the devil's schemes. We know our personal weaknesses where the enemy would try to enslave us again. And most of us are wise enough not to allow those things to survive in the fire of God's love. We also know that we have a responsibility to "stand in the gap" in prayer and intercession for saints and sinners alike, but like the story of Jehoshaphat, we must maintain our focus.

> Rest assured— God is MUCH bigger than the devil.

As the writer of Hebrews advises, "Let us fix our eyes on Jesus, the author and perfecter of our faith, who for the joy set before him endured the cross, scorning its shame, and sat down at the right hand of the throne of God" (Heb. 12:2, NIV). Our focus is on Jesus. He is the One who reigns—not the enemy. We ought not to waste our time on him but simply exalt the name of the Lord over every other name.

Read Philippians 2:9–11. The apostle Paul made it clear that Jesus holds all power and authority. What confession will all men and women ultimately be required to make about Him?

_____

_____

▲▲▲▲▲▲▲

Read Romans 10:13. The name of Jesus is higher than any other name. What promise is given to those who call on His name?

_____

_____

▲▲▲▲▲▲▲

Read Colossians 3:17. How did Paul instruct us to live in light of the power of Jesus' name?

_____

_____

▲▲▲▲▲▲▲

Another factor to consider is what we believe about Satan. The fact is... he is neither omnipotent nor omnipresent like God. God knows all things and is ubiquitous (can be everywhere simultaneously). The devil knows much less about everything and can personally be in only one location at a time. Wouldn't he be more concerned with toppling socioeconomic systems in places of strategic power than attending one of our worship services? The devil has more to bother with than people singing praises to God... or does he? (I've wondered about the strength of religious spirits. It seems they may be stronger than the average demonic force as they hang out in the praises of God's people.)

▲ ▲

The church's role in the earth is to consistently confirm that there is no other name, no other God and no other Lord!

▲ ▲

The simple truth revealed here is that of lordship! Who is really in charge? The One who created the heavens and the earth remains Lord and God regardless of any opposition. When we give thanks to Him, we reemphasize the fact that only Jesus Christ is Lord! The question of lordship is still being posed by the powers of darkness. The church's role in the earth is to consistently confirm that there is no other name, no other God and no other Lord!

We do that in our times of corporate worship. When we lift up the name of the Lord, we defy the rulers of the dark realm. There's no middle ground in the quest for establishing righteousness in the earth, and the war for ownership has concluded by Jesus' overwhelming victory! According to Psalm 24:1, "The earth is the LORD's, and all it contains." That means everything belongs to Him! The issue of rulership has long been established. Jesus rules! Satan does not! As God's voice in the earth, one of our responsibilities is to declare that simple truth and reinforce its ramifications through the worship of God.

When we worship Jesus, we are literally saying and singing, "You are God; there's no one else. Everything in heaven and

Worthy art Thou to take the book, and to break its seals; for Thou wast slain, and didst purchase for God with Thy blood men from every tribe and tongue and people and nation.

—Revelation 5:9

earth belongs to You and You alone. There's no power that compares to the One true, living God. You are worthy to receive all glory, honor and praise because You shed Your blood for us and redeemed us to God" (Rev. 5:9).

Let the high praises of God be in their mouth, and a two-edged sword in their hand, to execute vengeance on the nations, and punishments on the peoples; to bind their kings with chains, and their nobles with fetters of iron; to execute on them the judgment written; this is an honor for all His godly ones.

—Psalm 149:6–9

These verses from Psalm 149 offer clarity that there is an offensive function to the praise of God. High praises, swords, vengeance, punishments, chains and judgment sound rather severe for an average worship time! While the precise meaning of this passage may be somewhat obscure, there is obviously a connection between human praise and divine judgment. The singing of praise to God and the concept of warfare are intermingled. In light of this connection, I believe the Lord wants us to be aware of these principles to further the impact of punishment against evil forces through our worship.

A MIGHTY FORTRESS IS OUR GOD

The German reformer Martin Luther wrote this classic hymn in 1529—about twelve years after he nailed his famous ninety-five theses to the door of the church at the University of Wittenburg. The song came to him during a period of great conflict between Luther and the Roman Catholic Church. Considered one of the greatest hymns of all time, it is a confident expression of victory in the midst of conflict with evil.

A mighty fortress is our God,
A bulwark never failing;
Our helper He, amid the flood
Of mortal ills prevailing:
For still our ancient foe
Doth seek to work us woe;
His craft and power are great,
And armed with cruel hate
On earth is not his equal.

Did we in our own strength confide,
Our striving would be losing;
Were not the right Man on our side,
The Man of God's own choosing:
Dost ask who that may be?
Christ Jesus, it is He;
Lord Sabaoth, His name,
From age to age the same.
And He must win the battle.

And though this world, with devils filled,
Should threaten to undo us,
We will not fear, for God hath willed
His truth to triumph through us:
The Prince of Darkness grim,
We tremble not for him;
His rage we can endure,
For lo, his doom is sure,
One little word shall fell him.

That word above all earthly powers,
No thanks to them, abideth;
The Spirit and the gifts are ours
Through Him who with us sideth:
Let goods and kindred go,
This mortal life also;
The body they may kill:
God's truth abideth still,
His kingdom is forever.[1]

MILITANT PRAISE

Psalm 149 begins and ends with "Hallelujah!" As we saw in chapter 4, the term *hallelujah* is translated, "Praise the Lord." The word in its full form appears only in this psalm as a militant praise word in destruction of the ungodly. The Greek version, *alleluia*, appears only four times in the New Testament, and all four are located in Revelation 19 when God pours out judgment on His enemies.

Let's break down this word *hallelujah*. It's a compound word combining *praise (halal)* and *to God (Jah)*. Contrary to some schools of thought, *Jah* is not an abbreviation of *Jehovah*. *Jah* refers to the God who is. Jehovah refers to the God who will be, who is and who was. The use of "hallelu-jah" in praise and warfare is in the context of the present and NOW God. *Now* He judges. *Now* He renders recompense. *Now* He deals righteously with His enemies. *Now* He shows up to defend His people.

As you can see, it would be difficult to declare softly and sweetly a "hallelujah" song. The word must be used to rave, boast, shine forth and celebrate His glorious victory over all the powers of darkness. It lends itself to lots of sound and color!

Biblically, when the Lord "shows up" in time and history, His purpose is to pronounce blessing on the righteous and judgment on the wicked. Considering the various attributes of His character, the dominant understanding of God is that He is pleased with those who obey and displeased with those who don't! As a prophetic people, we function as a vehicle for these verdicts of God to be rendered against spiritual wickedness.

> As agents of reconciliation, we have the privilege of acting as coworkers with Him in the pursuit of reclaiming His possession and inheritance.

As agents of reconciliation, we have the privilege of acting as coworkers with Him in the pursuit of reclaiming His possession and inheritance. We accomplish this through our worship of Him as the Creator, Redeemer and owner. One job is to inform His creation that their sins are no longer counted against them. Jesus has taken the punishment for their disobedience and rejection of God's laws. Now they must simply accept and receive it.

Another job is to function as a tool to inform spiritual principalities that the authority of the Resurrection is far greater than any other event in history, and the presence of God in and through His people by the Spirit is inevitable.

Much has been said about the glory of the Lord and His manifested presence. We talk about it, pray about it and sing about it, often waiting in silence for long periods of time for God to show us His glory. When we've experienced some depth of His presence in worship, we usually leave knowing there is more. It creates an insatiable desire to be with Him and to know Him intimately.

Although there is sweetness in His embrace and tenderness

in His touch, there is an aspect of His glory and presence that is violent toward the enemy and includes the principle of warfare. Dr. David Blomgren, author of *Restoring Praise and Worship to the Church,* shares some personal insight:

> This is illustrated in Numbers 4:23 where the Lord is speaking to Moses about those who are appointed to be priests. He described them as all those who "enter in to perform the service…" The words "perform the service" are from Hebrew words which mean, literally, "fight the warfare." "Perform" is the translation of the Hebrew word *tsaba',* from which we get *sabbaoth* or hosts—as in Lord of Hosts, a name with strong military overtones…the priests entered into the holy place to fight a warfare.[2]

To bless the name of the Lord of Hosts in the performance of a service of worship is to invoke His wrath over His enemies. We, as His army, have the privilege of lifting praise to His name and then observing His name defeat spiritual powers of darkness. We can see results in the natural realm when battles are first fought in the spiritual realm.

A natural illustration of this can be seen in the children of Israel as they marched around the walls of Jericho under Joshua's leadership. Besides walking around the walls quietly for six days, they were required simply to raise a loud shout of praise on the seventh day. Benign though it may have been, it was a relatively painless prescription for victory. Following those simple instructions, they saw the hand of God destroy the walls of the city. Then they were able to conquer it.

So, was the shout *against* the enemy, or was it a vocal "amen" to the judgment of God? Regardless of the answer to that question, the fact remains—the walls came a-tumblin' down. God made His point clear when He responded in judgment to the shout!

You may ask, "Is our praise directed to God or against the enemy? Do we confess the lordship of Jesus Christ or confess our victory over darkness? Is He the object of our worship or the means to greater dimensions of authority against the enemy?" I don't believe the answers are yes to one and no to the other. The simultaneous achievement of exaltation and battle both occur in the primary elements of praise lifted to God.

Read Psalm 2:7–8. Why do we have the authority to reclaim all nations and people for Christ?

_____

_____

▲▲▲▲▲▲▲

Read Colossians 1:12–14. What did the apostle Paul say we are partakers of because of the blood of Christ?

_____

_____

▲▲▲▲▲▲▲

Read Hebrews 11:30. What do we need in order to see spiritual walls fall down?

_____

_____

▲▲▲▲▲▲▲

Another passage of great significance is in John's Revelation. Chapter 19 outlines a heavenly perspective of worship. Consider the following paraphrase of verses 1–6:

> *As the multitudes of heaven sang and worshiped the Lamb, the Holy One issued forth decrees against His enemies. As His words hit the target, accomplishing their purpose, the song swelled to a thunderous crescendo that shook the walls of the heavenly temple. The celestial hosts rejoiced with a loud noise in the righteousness of His judgments as once again the words of God were carried by messengers of brilliant light and poured out upon His demonic adversaries.*

We must look at heaven's model of worship. When the hosts of heaven worship, He dispatches His righteous judgments from heaven. That adds a whole new dimension to the purpose of corporate worship. Bringing heaven to earth is the reason Jesus came to earth. When we join with the saints of the ages, declaring the rule of God, heaven comes

> The simultaneous achievement of exaltation and battle both occur in the primary elements of praise lifted to God.

to earth and cosmic choruses of history past, present and future unite.

The apostle John heard the great multitude in heaven crying out with a loud voice in praise to God because God judged the great harlot who was corrupting the earth with her immoralities. (I believe the great harlot was a political and religious institution that was responsible for the blood of the martyrs.)

According to this account, God sent swift, definite and complete judgment to her on the earth for her corruption as the multitudes of heaven rejoiced in the righteous way God rendered His verdicts. This passage of Scripture, which is also known as the "Fourfold Hallelujah," includes the Marriage Supper of the Lamb as the final act of covenantal consummation after God's enemies are judged.

It appears that the body of Christ in heaven and on earth is essential to the heavenly design as God's vehicle for justice in the earth. To say that God has need of anything is silly, but He has chosen to work through His church, His body. He desires us to partner with Him so that He may gain access to the earth and its systems through a people who carry His name. God calls us to aggressively influence the spirit realm with the exaltation of Jesus' name while getting in on the action of heavenly violence against His enemies.

With regard to the judgments of God, Jesus alone rules, and there is no democracy in the kingdom! As the head of the church, He is entitled to call the shots as He chooses. And we as His body have the privilege of obeying the Ruler of all things. By virtue of our relationship to Him through His blood, we are authorized to carry out His judgments on principalities, powers and spiritual rulers of wickedness in high places.

OUR GOD

This contemporary chorus celebrates the awesome power of God over the nations, the elements and the demonic realm. Songs like this build our faith to believe that the gospel will triumph over even the most resistant cultures.

Our God, Jehovah is His name.
He's the God of heaven
And controls the rain.
Our God, Jehovah is His name.
Everything we do,
We do in the name of Jesus.

Elijah came to the mountain
To come against the prophets of Baal.
He looked at them with confidence
As he watched them scream and yell.
He said, "This drought is over,
Let's set the record straight.
There's no god but the one true God
Who controls the rain."

We are the church on the mountain.
We come against the gates of hell.
Declaring to the powers of darkness,
"You will not prevail."
We have an open heaven
Declared by the Lord who reigns.
There's no god but the one true God
Who controls the rain.[3]

SUPERNATURAL WEAPONS

To fully understand this concept we must continually remind ourselves that our warfare is not against flesh and blood. We are not fighting people! The weapons we use are not of this natural world, but they are powerfully supernatural to the point of annihilating strongholds of darkness and demonically inspired philosophies of men.

We wage war in the spirit through prayer and worship with the sword of the Spirit, the Word of God. When we engage the enemy through these mediums, we are to tear down arguments and every pretension that sets itself up against the reality of the knowledge of God. We are to take captive every thought and make it obedient to Christ (2 Cor. 10:4–5). We are to do this not just in our own minds, but also in the hearts and minds of

> For the weapons of our warfare are not of the flesh, but divinely powerful for the destruction of fortresses. We are destroying speculations and every lofty thing raised up against the knowledge of God, and we are taking every thought captive to the obedience of Christ.
> —2 Corinthians 10:4–5

those who are disobedient to Christ because of demonic influence. It's the god of this age that blinds men's hearts to the gospel (2 Cor. 4:3–4).

One acclamation of the early church was "Maranatha!" To them it meant much more than "The Lord is coming." A more literal translation of this phrase can be, "The Lord comes swiftly to judge His enemies!" When the first-century church would gather to worship, combined with psalms, hymns and spiritual songs, they would seize the opportunity to declare the lordship of Jesus with this acclamation. They understood the issue of the day to be lordship and ownership.

With a greeting and salutation like that to open and close each worship gathering, one would quickly view God as One who does not turn a blind eye or a deaf ear to the exploitation of the oppressed. "'Vengeance is mine, I will repay,' says the LORD" takes on a uniquely different flavor. The retribution of God was recognized as inevitable, and they participated in its preparation with the term "Maranatha!"

Initially it wasn't illegal to be a Christian in the first century. People worshiped many gods, as was their custom. Adding Jesus Christ to the list wasn't an issue. The problem came when the early Christians declared that there was *no other God* (especially not Caesar) and no other way to Him but through Jesus! Again, lordship and ownership were being challenged.

Even so today! Why does the enemy try to stop the praise of God? Simply because he is reminded once again that he lost the war! It is imperative that we practice now what we believe about the future. The fact that Jesus reigns through His people today is something that can be celebrated. For us, the concept of "Maranatha!" is not just subjective principles based on centuries of conjecture regarding God's intentions. Rather it is an objective certainty as we see God judging His enemies in our day.

Spiritual forces in specific realms or arenas are best defeated by consistent declarations of the truth rather than by a defiant personal address. In essence, declaring truth is the fundamental function of the sword of the Spirit. God's Word is ultimate truth, and it must be proclaimed. If indeed the

> And even if our gospel is veiled, it is veiled to those who are perishing, in whose case the god of this world has blinded the minds of the unbelieving, that they might not see the light of the gospel of the glory of Christ, who is the image of God.
> —2 Corinthians 4:3–4

church is God's voice in the earth to communicate truth, we must develop our ability to declare and demonstrate that truth effectively.

▲▲
Spiritual forces in specific realms or arenas are best defeated by consistent declarations of the truth rather than by a defiant personal address.
▲▲

The most powerful truth of all time that the church is honored to declare is that Jesus Christ is Lord! There is nothing more eternal in prophetic significance than that. Sadly, the church in its present state has virtually underestimated the power of this truth. We've tended to gravitate to things more sensational to feel effective in the spirit, often missing the most basic of all spiritual points. We must get back to a simple understanding that there is nothing more threatening to the powers of darkness than for a group of believers who know their God to declare the lordship of Jesus over their personal situations, their cities, their communities and the entire earth.

Read 2 Corinthians 10:3. When engaging in spiritual battle, what do we have to be careful not to walk in?

_____

_____

▲▲▲▲▲▲▲

Read Luke 4:18. Proclaiming God's Word is integral to being victorious in spiritual battle. What prophetic declarations did Jesus make from the Book of Isaiah?

_____

_____

▲▲▲▲▲▲▲

Read Ephesians 6:17. The apostle Paul specifically defined what the sword of the Spirit is. What is it?

_____

_____

▲▲▲▲▲▲▲

I remember when the phrase "Jesus is Lord" began to be used as a catch phrase by Christians during the Jesus Movement of the late sixties. Although it has continued to a degree as one of those "Christianese" sayings, in most circles it has lost its prophetic edge. The simplicity of the expression has been diminished in significance to an afterthought or a "filler phrase" with little credence. Anemic and clichéd as it may seem to say or sing, "Jesus is Lord," it is still one of the most powerful weapons of the church against the forces of the enemy when used with conviction and Holy Ghost fervor.

The plan of God for His people is prophetic in nature. Not only does He want *to* speak to His people, but He also desires to speak *through* His people to the inhabitants of the earth and to the powers of darkness in the spirit realm! Our corporate gatherings are much more than individuals coming together to joyously sing songs, fervently pray and recite some form of liturgy. We literally become the body of Christ in function to facilitate the work of the Spirit as we declare eternal truths about the lordship, authority and dominion of Jesus.

Because the church is God's vehicle to infiltrate the earth with His truth, we must have a spiritual plan to do so regularly rather than just randomly screaming attacks of hyper-energy blasts into the heavenlies. Let us allow the truth of God to flow through us prophetically and consistently, declaring the lordship of Jesus. If we don't, who will?

Throughout history, the Lord has consistently searched for a living organism He could use to demonstrate His covenantal faithfulness in the earth. When He spoke the Word, worlds came into existence. The power of His creative Word (Jesus Christ) is the same today as He continues to locate people who will speak it and truly believe it. Thus the power of the Word is in the *speaking* and in the *living*.

Confession has been a part of the Christian faith since the days of the founding fathers. The recitation of oaths and creeds date back to the early centuries. Over the past twenty-five years, we've seen the abuses of inappropriate confession through leaders with mostly good intentions. Many have "confessed" the Word of God and used it for personal gain over and

> Let us allow the truth of God to flow through us prophetically and consistently, declaring the lordship of Jesus.

Therefore, holy brethren, partakers of a heavenly calling, consider Jesus, the Apostle and High Priest of our confession.

—Hebrews 3:1

above God's purpose. Be that as it may, let us consider the truth of holy and Spirit-led confessions that are based on God's eternal wisdom.

Biblical confession is "saying what God says." The Greek word for *confession* is *homologia*. Since Jesus is the High Priest of our confession, He can make perfect intercession for me before the Father when I agree with what He says about my circumstances and myself (Heb. 3:1). So, when I come to Him personally, emptying my soul of the fear, pain and shame of life's current situations, I must say the same thing that heaven says in order to receive His fullness of grace.

With regard to corporate worship, we must worship according to the reality of what heaven is saying about Jesus, the power of His blood and the authority of His kingdom. If we allow our natural minds alone—which are bound to the temporal, experiential realm—to attempt faith-filled confessions, that's soul power. With that, His kingdom cannot come easily, nor can His will be done in or through us. We must agree with His position of kingship rather than our experience.

In this prophetic sense, we declare God's current truth, changeless in its existence and supreme in its authority, which has the power to dismantle the kingdoms of this world and dethrone the rulers of wickedness in high places. Even now, those who believe their praises make a difference are proclaiming the manifold wisdom of God throughout the earth: "The wisdom which none of the rulers of this age has understood; for if they understood it, they would not have crucified the Lord of glory" (1 Cor. 2:8).

Why not? Because since Christ's resurrection the multiplication factor has exceeded Satan's imagination. Satan was clueless that the resurrection of Jesus would cause his plans to disintegrate. Had he and his minions thought it through, they would have immediately aborted their plans to kill Jesus in the first place. (I've heard it said that from the time Jesus crushed Satan's head under His foot, the devil has had brain damage.) Through the centuries an unfathomable exponential number of believers have been "prophesying" God's current Word in the worship of Jesus Christ, which has and still is displacing forces of evil in the spiritual realm!

As God's prophetic people who are familiar with His Word, we foretell the future according to the Scriptures and forthtell His forever current words in the life of Christ. So let us confess and declare with confidence through our worship that:

▲ Jesus *is* truly Lord and reigns over all the earth from the right hand of God, regardless of what we see with our natural eyes.

▲ The complete redemptive work of the cross *is* enough to save every man from hell, regardless of how foolish the message.

▲ The same God who raised Jesus from the dead *is* the One who rules over the destinies of men and nations, regardless of the seeming hopelessness of human tyranny.

▲ The Holy Spirit *is* definitely at work in the earth moving men to faith and obedience, leading them to find God's will in His Word, regardless of the floundering that many experience in life.

▲ We are the church who believe in Jesus as the Son of God, proclaiming forgiveness of sin and reconciliation to God regardless of the opposition to our commission by the spirit of this age.[4]

Paul writes, "Oh, the depth of the riches both of the wisdom and knowledge of God! How unsearchable are His judgments and unfathomable His ways" (Rom. 11:33). What an incredibly strategic and well-thought-out plan of God to utilize the praises of His people to wreak havoc with the dark side.

LET'S TALK ABOUT IT

▲ When we are fighting spiritual battles in prayer, why is it important to focus on Jesus, not the enemy?

_____

_____

▲▲▲▲▲▲▲

▲ Describe a spiritual battle over which you recently experienced victory.

_____

_____

▲▲▲▲▲▲▲

▲ Over what areas of your life do you feel you should declare "Jesus is Lord!"?

_____

_____

▲▲▲▲▲▲▲

▲ What lesson can we learn from the biblical examples of His people singing praises to God during times of warfare?

_____

_____

▲▲▲▲▲▲▲

YOUR TIME WITH GOD

Father, I declare that Jesus is Lord over every situation in my life—my personal life, my family, my work and my church. When I face spiritual attacks, remind me of the truth of Your Word so that I can declare it over the situation and against the enemy. I thank You that Satan was defeated when You died on the cross, and that I can claim that victory every day for my family and me. Amen.

CHAPTER TEN

One River— Many Streams of Worship

T HE SWOLLEN MISSISSIPPI RIVER REACHED FLOOD STAGE FOR THE THIRD TIME IN A CEN- TURY. People living on its banks were astounded at the amount of rising water as daily they waited for the announce- ment to evacuate. Their fears rose as the water rose. Leaving the farm was a difficult decision to make—for four generations they had faithfully worked the fields. The creeks and streams that fed the mighty Mississippi were bursting their sides in an attempt to reach the main flow. It seemed to be a mad-dash race to an indefinite liquid finish line. It was only a matter of time before the weather up north forced the people down south to deal with the aftermath of the coming torrent—and nothing could stop it!

For years, civilizations have been built on the banks of rivers. Flowing water was a positive sign of health and vitality, making agriculture possible and facilitating trade with other cities. Water has been viewed as the source of life—it is not possible to exist without it for more than a few days. Men have attempted to tame the flow of water from the beginning with dams and gates. Modern man has even succeeded in harnessing the power of major waterways to provide an energy supply for entire areas of the country.

One of the greatest challenges is getting the water to go where you want it. Water will flow to the lowest places where gravity is the greatest. And it would seem those are the places that need it most. But the larger the river, the greater the dif- ficulty controlling it. Rushing water cannot be stopped unless man-made devices are constructed to manage and direct it.

Psalm 46:4–5 says, "There is a river whose streams make

IN THIS CHAPTER YOU WILL DISCOVER THAT...

▲ Our methods may differ, but our goal is the same.

▲ The Creator has designed a mosaic of comprehensive tex- tures together in one magnifi- cent array of splendid brilliance.

glad the city of God, the holy dwelling places of the Most High. God is in the midst of her, she will not be moved." Interesting statement, since Jerusalem, the city of God, had no river. Perhaps the psalmist was speaking of the heavenly bounty of God's blessings. Certainly he had seen enough of those through the years.

The river of God, the supernatural flow of the Spirit, the creative aspect of His presence and the knowledge of His glory cannot be stifled. "For the earth will be filled with the knowledge of the glory of the LORD, as the waters cover the sea" (Hab. 2:14).

Expect to see the kingdom growing and the river flowing until it fills all the earth with the knowledge of His glory. That's the power of kingdom creativity at work through His people in the earth!

The river that flows through the kingdom or the city of God is made up of many different "streams." The inference in Psalm 46:4 is that God dwells in the holy places of the streams that feed the river. To think that one individual group has the full revelation of God's heart is absurd and smacks of cultic segregation. There must be both an acknowledgment and an acceptance of the Holy Spirit's work of revealing Jesus through each stream in order for us to have a broader picture of God's purpose in the earth.

> One of the greatest challenges is getting the water to go where you want it.

As history so beautifully illustrates, the creative work of God's Spirit leads men and women to accomplish things for His glory. When we view His Word as the ultimate guideline for all decisions, He grants us the ability and freedom to interpret the details based on our knowledge of Him. As much as we may like or dislike the concept, God does use an individual's personality, natural abilities, strengths and weaknesses to plow ground for planting spiritual seed. The following they gather is usually people with similar tastes and perspectives. We are all products of teaching, training and experience.

In his book *Illustrations for Preaching and Teaching,* Craig Brian Larson tells the following story:

Frasier of Lisuland in northern Burma translated the Scriptures into the Lisu language and then left a young fellow with the task of teaching the people to read. When he returned six months later, he found three students and the teacher seated around a table, with the Scriptures opened in front of the teacher. When the students each read, they left the Bible where it was. The man on the left read it sideways, the man on the right read it sideways but from the other side, and the man across from the teacher read it upside down. Since they always occupied the same chairs, that's how each had learned to read, and that's how each thought the language was written.

We, too, can be like that. When we learn something from only one perspective, we may think it's the only perspective. Sometimes it's good to change seats to assume a different perspective on the same truth.[1]

This story is indicative of our personal perspectives, which are often rigid, but neither right nor wrong. This is true for our "methods" of ministry in the kingdom as well. The point is, we each have a job to do in the kingdom. Our methods may differ but our goal is the same. If we can release one another to flow freely in our respective elements, we will make greater headway on the task ahead.

Read 1 Corinthians 12:20–21. What did the apostle Paul say about our different functions in the body of Christ and how we should interact with each other?

_____

_____

▲▲▲▲▲▲▲

Read 1 Corinthians 12:26. What happens to the body of Christ if one member suffers?

_____

_____

▲▲▲▲▲▲▲

Read 1 Corinthians 12:28. Who appointed the different roles that are important to the spiritual health of the church?

_____

_____

▲▲▲▲▲▲▲

The way I see things may be completely different from the way you do. Despite our perspective differences, that doesn't have to isolate us into different camps as being right or wrong. If so, we become imprisoned by the subconscious fear of inevitable challenge when we consider others' belief systems about God. Actually, when we drop our defenses, we are presented with opportunities to experience truth and to express it differently.

In a healthy body, the fingers cannot do what the toes do. Nor can the liver do the gallbladder's job. Every part is important to the overall function of the body. The way we perceive God, His voice and the leading of His Spirit is what makes the body of Christ so intricately complex. Each member plays an important role in the whole manifestation of Christ in the earth. And the various aspects of God's personality are portrayed in the assortment of vessels through which He is permitted to flow.

Growing up in a relatively large family by today's standards, I am the fifth of six children. All of us, though distinctly different in personality type, gender and life goals, look very much alike, with fair hair, fair skin and blue eyes. Even our perspectives of life are similar because we were raised under the same roof by the same parents with the same basic moral values and experiences. We have a frightening amount of similarities, yet we are definitely different to the point of being terminally unique.

▲▲

Finally we're beginning to see the blessing of God on many of our unified kingdom efforts as the church lays aside petty differences and chooses to walk hand in hand with those of other families, clans, groups, tribes and personality types.

▲▲

The essence of predominant features characterizing families can be found in churches and organizations as well, as is evidenced in the early church when Paul tried to settle quarrels between those who said, "'I am of Paul' and 'I of Apollos' and 'I of Cephas' and 'I of Christ'" (1 Cor. 1:12).

Many of those disciples were brought into the kingdom via the inimitable ministry of a particular individual, which gave them a sense of "belonging to" him. In no way was Paul trying to pull these people out of their families, groups or clans. His point was that the body of Christ was united under the shadow of the cross.

The same is true today in the variety of personalities that characterize the vast assortment of camps and streams. The unity of the Spirit that is taking place in our generation is phenomenal. Finally we're beginning to see the blessing of God on many of our unified kingdom efforts as the church lays aside petty differences and chooses to walk hand in hand with those of other families, clans, groups, tribes and personality types.

Globally, the unique difference that each local expression of Christ's body offers is genuinely validated by the illustration in John's revelation. He saw nations, tribes, tongues and ethnic groups worshiping around the throne *together*—each in its own language. Picture this display of colorful cultures before the presence of God! The Creator has designed a mosaic of comprehensive textures full of His glory, joined together in one magnificent spray of splendid brilliance. Incredible creativity!

PSALM 122:1-5

The psalm about Jerusalem, the heavenly city of God, foreshadows the church—which is made up of many "tribes" that represent various denominations within the body of Christ. God's desire is that the many-membered body of Christ walk in unity.

I was glad when they said to me,
"Let us go to the house of the Lord."
Our feet are standing
Within your gates, O Jerusalem,
Jerusalem, that is built
As a city that is compact together;
To which the tribes go up, even the tribes of the Lord—
An ordinance for Israel—
To give thanks to the name of the Lord.
For there thrones were set for judgment,
The thrones of the house of David.

A GOD OF VARIETY

Do you ever get bored with the "same old thing"? Our lives are peppered with new things from time to time, but our daily and weekly rituals of getting up, going to work, coming home, eating dinner and engaging in the same activities over and over can tend to anesthetize us to the rare and "special" events that keep life interesting. Sometimes we need to get off our mental stationary bicycle and branch out to a real walk in the park (with or without the dog). Of course there's nothing wrong with the daily disciplines of faithfulness to family life and your job. Still, I find it necessary to break up my monotony with spontaneity.

I get weary of eating the same kind of foods as well. My wife is aware of this and has taken pity on me to the point of becoming a fabulous cook over the years. Though tightly budgeted, she sees to it that we eat a variety of what I call "designer" foods—not just the stock, "B-flat" meat, potatoes, vegetables and casseroles, but a culinary cuisine of multi-ethnic flavors. I can't tell you how many times she's come up with a new dish... by mistake. Throwing this and that together and *voilá*... "Creation *á la* Laurie." To her sincere credit, most of the time it's pretty good, and the kids have grown accustomed to a plethora of tastes. If variety is indeed the spice of life, then my family enjoys the garlic, the basil and sometimes Brussels sprout experiences.

I think the Lord is just as moved with delight at the varied diet we offer Him in our worship styles and flavors. How refreshing it must be to Him for us to grasp a truth about God, create a means by which to express it and then present it to Him as an offering. He has created us with such unique personalities and giftings to portray the vastness of His creativity in the earth.

The various streams of worship music today aptly reflect the perspectives and values of the leadership gifts they represent. A flavorful combination of merged musical styles can add an entirely new dimension of expression to an otherwise average worship gathering.

As we enjoy the multiple facets of God in worship, our

celebration of Him is just as multifaceted through the beauty of music, art, prayer and Scripture reading. Yet at times it is overwhelming to conceive that He is Creator and Redeemer, the victorious Champion, the Good Shepherd, the awesome God and the Lover of our souls. How do we worship a God like this effectively? The divine tension between these clearly descriptive titles and characteristics serves as a continual reminder of our inability to capture all of who He is in a single worship gathering within the walls of our limited scope of reference. We must regularly ask Him what part of His *all-in-all* character He would like us to experience.

Though you may not be a worship leader, you're probably reading this book because you've been sensitized to the rising awareness of worship issues today. Or perhaps you just want to know God in a deeper way by learning more about this vast topic. In any case, worship music is playing an enormous role today in connecting us to the supernatural power of God.

What we feed ourselves becomes part of us. The famous quip of today, "You are what you eat," means a lot more than, "Don't eat carcinogenic foods." More than a big "DON'T," it is an extra important "DO"! Our bodies need a balanced diet from the four basic food groups to maintain strength and health. Though we may not be particularly fond of green vegetables, Mother taught us that we'd live longer if we had a few helpings each week. And don't forget the fiber! It helps to get rid of the things your body doesn't need.

Then there's physical exercise! For many of us, it's a discipline we know we must endure to feel better. Yet it has still not become a part of our lives the way it should. The time commitment is usually something we can't afford, and the rigor of the "no pain, no gain" idea is completely unappealing. But as nutritionists and dietitians tell us, a good diet without exercise is only half beneficial.

Feeding and nurturing the spirit man is just as crucial as taking care of the natural man. The diet and exercise of devotion through worship and prayer must be just as balanced for us to gain revelation and understanding of God and His ways. Still, regularly we seem to graze in a "safe zone."

> Feeding and nurturing the spirit man is just as crucial as taking care of the natural man.

We comfort ourselves with a certain kind of surrounding that fits our character and personality preference. It's typically safer than to broaden our proverbial horizons and embrace things that don't quite fit into our spiritually aesthetic easy chairs with the attached ottoman.

For example: If my spiritual experience began with an intimate, informal gathering with no instruments, I would tend to find that familiar and comforting. If I find that my heart is stirred most by music that reflects Jesus' shepherd heart, I'll probably be less interested in singing about His righteous rule over the nations. If my view of God is through the colors of stained glass and liturgical vestments, it may be difficult to connect with Him at a contemporary Christian Rave. Whatever the case, there's room for growth and change in our diet and exercise regimen.

Read Hebrews 5:12–14. Watching our "spiritual diet" is important to our growth in the Lord. What did the writer mean when he told believers they needed to be eating "solid food"?

_____

_____

▲▲▲▲▲▲▲

Read 1 Timothy 4:7. Paul also talked about spiritual exercise. What did he say we should exercise ourselves toward?

_____

_____

▲▲▲▲▲▲▲

Read 1 Timothy 4:8. How did he say this will benefit us?

_____

_____

▲▲▲▲▲▲▲

If we stop to think about the worship music utilized in our local congregations, there are several points to consider as we ask some pertinent questions.

1. *Vision*—What are we to do as a community of believers? What has God said to our leaders that we have agreed

with and have joined hands in covenant to do?

2. *Identity*—Who are we as a local congregation? Of what kinds of people are we comprised? What is our predominant ethnic origin, and how do we intend to preserve the redemptive value of our culture?

3. *Target audience*—From a position of our identity and culture as a church, we should be able to determine a target group of people to minister to. What is the personality profile of the congregation with which we are joined? Are they predominantly blue-collar workers, young urban professionals, single, married with children, city folk, country folk, teens, college/career or a blended variety? Determining the strengths and weaknesses of a local fellowship narrows down or broadens out our worship repertoire.

4. *Purpose*—What is our purpose? That is, why do we do what we do? In a recent poll, 90 percent of Christians surveyed believe the church exists to meet their needs. But 89 percent of clergy surveyed believe the church exists to reach the world.[2] The margin of philosophical gray area here is huge and must be shrunk before being effective.

5. *Goals and objectives*—An established purpose will evolve from our goals and objectives. These are the practical ways in which we can fulfill our purpose. These goals and objectives will also help us embrace our particular distinctives as a group of believers in a specific location. If one goal is to reach the community, how do we intend to do that?

6. *Musical style*—Musical style is essentially driven by preference—not conviction! Each local culture must respond to God with the musical flavor that best suits their group. Style in many congregations is often a reflection of the worship team itself and the musicality of the worship leader in particular. Some musicians get comfortable with the "groove" of music

they've labored hard to achieve and find their leadership flourishes best there.

Church statistics show that the three main drawing cards to a local fellowship are the music, the preaching and the body life. If the worship leader is relatively comfortable primarily with one flavor of musical style, he can assume with a guarantee that the people to whom he ministers the most are those with similar tastes. The compatibility of the worship leader's musical style and the congregation's response is normally dependent on the ability of leadership to palatably present new things without sacrificing continuity or personality.

Taking into consideration the cultural shift over the past three decades and the personality makeup of your congregation, does the worship "style" of your church reflect the vision of the house, your pastor and the people? With regard to form and content, are you focusing on acts of worship in the congregational setting or a prevailing lifestyle of worship?

With regard to identity and comfort, tradition is an enormous factor in what dictates appropriate style. The values of a local congregation will be evidenced by where funds are invested. Musically, if the style is traditional, the piano and organ will be well taken care of. On the other hand if the style is contemporary, keyboards, guitars and midi equipment will be the focus.

O CHURCH OF GOD, UNITED

This classic Methodist hymn was written before its time. It seems to foreshadow a day when the church will overcome all racial and denominational barriers.

O Church of God, united
To serve one common Lord,
Proclaim to all one message,
With hearts in glad accord.
Christ ever goes before us;
We follow day by day
With strong and eager footsteps
Along the upward way.

From every land and nation
The ordered ranks appear;
To serve one valiant Leader
They come from far and near.
They chant their one confession,
They praise one living Lord,
And place their sure dependence
Upon His saving Word.

Though creeds and tongues may differ
They speak, O Christ, of Thee;
And in Thy loving Spirit
We shall one people be
Lord, may our faithful service
And singleness of aim
Proclaim to all the power
Of Thy redeeming name.

May Thy great prayer be answered
That we may all be one,
Close bound, by love united
In Thee, God's blessed Son;
To bring a single witness,
To make the pathway bright,
That souls which grope in darkness
May find the one true Light.[3]

TRADITION AND THE FUTURE

1. The oral tradition

Until five hundred years ago, speaking was the basic means of communication in what is called the "oral tradition." There was nothing to record…no information or wisdom to disseminate but the memories of the community elders, musicians and storytellers. History and important information were passed on to the next generation and kept alive through stories, parables and myths celebrated in festivals and ceremonial rituals. The ancient Egyptian and Hebrew cultures, the early church and medieval society were birthed in this tradition.

For more than a thousand years the spoken word had

power in the oral tradition. Truth was directly tied to relationships within the tribe or village. Many things in the small community were shared together, like homes, meals and child rearing. Due to the unwritten word, "Most of the Bible existed first in oral form and depended for its survival on a circle of people who memorized it, recited it and handed down to successive generations."[4]

The liturgical tradition of worship was birthed from the oral tradition of communication, and the message of the gospel was communicated through reenactment and symbolism. Rich in symbolic imagery, the Eucharist became the focus of reality in worship. Because of relational upbringing, people could connect the act of the Table with Jesus' words: "Do this in remembrance of Me."

2. The print tradition

Though the Chinese had developed a way to create paper in the second century, it took thirteen hundred years for the revelation to reach Europe. By the fifteenth century, the printing press was invented, and the printed page revolutionized Western communication. Paper was much easier and cheaper to make than parchment, and it could be produced more uniformly. Principle and purpose characterized this tradition, and cognitive thought was an essential element of intelligence.

Print fueled the Renaissance, and the Reformation launched modernity emphasizing reading, writing, understanding and logical reason. The print revolution and the "thinking" form of communication helped to shape Protestant worship. The approach to worship became focused on mentally understanding the propositions of faith and acting on that knowledge. Later, reformed theology beginning with Martin Luther shifted its main focus from the Eucharist to include singing and preaching.

3. The electronic tradition

The telephone was a monumental creation toward the end of the nineteenth century. And through the rise of communication techniques and electronics, the audiovisual tradition erupted in the early 1950s with television. Hearing the word and seeing the images on the screen created an entirely new genre of interaction and entertainment.

Through developing technology, a new worship tradition was formed—Pentecostalism. Even though the Pentecostal experience had been around for several decades, it won greater notoriety through the television ministries of Rex Humbard and Oral Roberts. Progressing into the 1980s, other televangelists came into view with their own programs. Unfortunately, casting aside theology and appealing to the sensational, many outgrew their usefulness to the kingdom and became bywords.

4. The digital age

We have entered a new era of digital communication combining ingredients of the other three mediums: audio, graphic, text *and data,* keeping them separate but allowing unlimited combinations.

> It is the first-time-in-history harnessing of atoms, electrons, quarks and their binary units of information. That harnessing takes the form of compact discs (CDs), calculators, fiber-optic cables, cellular phones, digital video discs (DVDs) and the ubiquitous computer and the global interconnection and interaction of computers into what we call the Internet.[5]

The Internet is the fastest-growing communication device in the history of the world. Dennis Jones, president and CEO of Federal Express, predicts it will soon become the "center of the universe."

A new church is rising from this paradigm with postmodern affectations. No longer can they be categorized in the old way. They don't fit into molds or models like the churches characteristic of the last decade. Responding to a youth culture that has chosen to abandon the absolutes of society, many are becoming strong beacons of Christian faith by sharing their radical witness.

In today's digital age, there is a growing awareness of God's purposes through the differences we are able to offer one another. Because our culture is in transition, morphing into an entirely new society with new values, customs, patterns and paradigms, the challenge is to protect our distinctive tradition while exploring variety.

Through various related groups and networks, music and worship have played a significant role in the development of each group's personality profile. It is stimulating to discover God's redemptive gift in each individual clan.

As you're probably aware, at your local Christian bookstore it is possible to find every kind of worship music to fit any kind of taste. The multihued spectrum includes everything from fifth-century Gregorian Chants to Gospel to Emo/Indy Punk Praise. It's almost essential to have a "Christian Worship Music Discovery Channel" available to help us sift through the massive amount of products.

Yet, once the fundamental focus of a fellowship is determined, it's easier to accept the arena of taste, style and texture of that local expression. Understanding the redemptive heart of God as expressed through various musical genres has helped many grasp their respective purpose and gives license to cross over the boundaries between them without feeling disloyal to any particular stream.

As much as we enjoy the flavors of today's current ministry, obviously it has not always been like this. Those who knew there must be more in their experience with God have paved the road from yesteryear through the centuries to today with lots of blood, sweat and tears. The tenacity of our fathers in the faith has demonstrated there's more to personal worship than what the previous generation had prescribed.

In our generation there are those who are attempting the same. Many are writing music that depicts the ebb and flow of their personal experience with God, while others are conceptualizing the sentiment of entire groups of people. At any rate, the perspective of such groups offers a vast smorgasbord of style that will appeal to every heart desiring to honor God with songs from the Spirit.

Historically, the musical revolution of the 1960s produced a whole new arena of identification with current culture. With its immoral themes of sex, drugs and rock-'n'-roll, God was unwilling to let an entire generation plunge headlong into a radical "non-destiny" without redemption.

Nikolai Lenin (1870–1924) made a profound statement around the turn of the twentieth century. He stated, "One quick way to destroy a society is through its music."[6]

Be that as it may, from the turn of the sixties to the seventies, the Jesus Movement produced a brand-new group of young participants who, with their zeal and vigor, decided that God could redeem the musical style of their era. The heart of worship they longed to express was birthed from a culturally counterfeit consciousness. Albeit subconscious in many respects, the youth of that day saw that Jesus could be glorified by transferring holy passion to the musical styles that once glorified the flesh, the world and the devil.

Maranatha! Music was born, as were other companies choosing to capture the new youthful, vibrant sound of folk-rock style worship. Maranatha! was one of the first recording companies to offer the church contemporary worship music that was easily accessible for congregational use. From the studios in southern California came their Praise series that has blessed the church for over two decades.

Not long afterward came the sound of the Vineyard. The evolution of worship music from the Vineyard stream, founded by the late John Wimber, has consistently reflected his heart for people to know the Father intimately. The notoriety of this music has spread rampantly throughout the world as a primary source for intimate worship.

One of the earmarks of the Vineyard movement has been the emphasis on the Father's house and the return of the prodigal. Thematically, it has a warm appeal to those who have been fatherless or have lacked a healthy image of a father figure in their lives. The Vineyard has provided us with that intimate mood in the presence of God, as is evidenced on their recordings by a sincere passion for knowing Him and lavishing love on Him in the secret place.

In our day, with so many nonexistent, absent or abusive fathers, thanks be to God for the worship writers in this stream who have heard the cry of a fatherless generation and combined it with the loving response of the Father's nurturing heart.

From a prominent composer in the Vineyard clan come these words about purpose and focus.

> The Vineyard will never depart from the value of intimate communion with God. But we can't forget the overall biblical definition of worship—to give our whole lives as an offering to God. If my life isn't pointed toward helping people, then my musical worship has very little meaning."[7]

In the early 1980s, two men who had been associated with *New Wine Magazine* had an experience with God in worship. They soon realized the need for live, recorded worship music in the Christian market. They answered a call from God to capture that element of live praise and worship on tape, and in 1985 they founded Integrity Music.

Besides giving us a glimpse into what the Holy Spirit was doing around the globe in worship, a redemptive gift in these streams of worship music is that of a cross-denominational effect. It seemed the entire born-again world had the same hunger for a new sound, a new experience and a new presence of God in worship.

The 1990s brought works of renewal and sparks of revival with music from the United Kingdom and Australia. Again, another fresh sound that captured the genuineness of hearts longing for God without all the flash of the previous decade. Styles changed once more as youth culture and subcultures proliferated the Christian music scene.

▲▲▲

God's intention in His sovereign wisdom and power is continuing to pour out revelation of Himself into every available pot and pan for the purpose of overflowing the earth with the knowledge of His glory.

▲▲▲

Today in this new millennium, the cry is still the same. We know we can't remain the same as the previous generation. In fact, many millennials do not trust the previous generation to lead them into the future. They feel alone to face the world. This is not a new feeling by any means. Many of our predecessors felt the same way, which is why the pioneering spirit has been a strong characteristic of each successive generation for the past century.

Still, the rich deposits of grace in worship revelation as expressed through these various avenues serve to unite the body of Christ by granting us a scope far beyond our personal limits. The perspectives we hold of God and His truth have come to us in a variety of ways—through our environment, upbringing, circumstances, teaching, training and personal revelation in prayer and worship.

In these days where knowledge has increased, the number of vehicles for expressing and communicating that knowledge has also increased. God's intention in His sovereign wisdom and power is continuing to pour out revelation of Himself into every available pot and pan for the purpose of overflowing the earth with the knowledge of His glory.

ALL OVER THE WORLD

This contemporary chorus declares with prophetic power that all the divisions in the church are falling because God's Spirit is being outpoured.

Your river is flowing,
Your presence has come.
Your Spirit is moving
All over the world.
You're touching the nations,
You're bringing Your love.
Your Spirit is moving
All over the world.

All over the world,
All over the world,
Your Spirit is moving
All over the world.

Your banner is lifted
Your praises are sung.

Your Spirit is moving
All over the world.
Divisions are falling,
You're making us one,
Your Spirit is moving
All over the world.[8]

We are living in incredible times, as the full expression of God in the earth is greater now than ever. If true worship is in spirit and truth, should we not make ourselves aware of every possible resource so that our hearts can be free to know and love God more fully?

Similar to the question that was asked by our parents thirty years ago or so—"What is this world coming to?"—there is much discussion about what the complexion of the current Praise and Worship movement will be within the next ten years. As difficult as this may be to answer, it is apparent that the next generation is receiving enough revelation from God to carry the torch of His presence into the next segment of this millennium. Though musical styles will change and methods of communication will expand, our prayers are that the hearts of the youth will accommodate the call of God to take the worship of His name to a higher and deeper level than we experienced.

As we've dawned the twenty-first century, the Holy Spirit reminds us that redemption draws near in the form of another visitation from God, which will produce an overflowing harvest of souls into the kingdom. Just as it's been with each previous move of God, *purging and preparation* is the call of today. As the Lord prepares the hearts of His people through repentance and the return to holiness, worship in His house is taking on new dimensions that will unite the body of Christ around the globe for the tasks at hand and ahead. The sense of community through worship is being built by the hand of God to prove to the earth that there *IS* a God who abides in the praises of His people.

For those living under His shadow and loving His appearing, our response to the awesome flood tide of coming glory and the fire of His presence is, "Even so, come, Lord Jesus!"

> The sense of community through worship is being built by the hand of God to prove to the earth that there IS a God who abides in the praises of His people.

LET'S TALK ABOUT IT

▲ Why is it important that God created us different from one another?

_____

_____

▲▲▲▲▲▲▲

▲ What can we learn from each other's differences?

_____

_____

▲▲▲▲▲▲▲

▲ How can we better learn to appreciate other church models, liturgies and styles of worship?

_____

_____

▲▲▲▲▲▲▲

▲ Describe a time when God taught you something through another member of the body of Christ who had a different perspective than you.

_____

_____

▲▲▲▲▲▲▲

YOUR TIME WITH GOD

Father, thank You for the diversity You've created in the body of Christ so that we can better reach our world for You. Help me to be more open with and learn more from my brothers and sisters in the Lord who come from different backgrounds and styles of worship. Help me to find ways to join hands with others so that we can, together, reach more people for You. As we worship together, inhabit our praises and empower us to impact this generation for You. Amen.

Notes

Chapter 1
Who We Worship

1. Judson Cornwall, *Philosophy of Worship* (Columbus, GA: Christian Life Publications, 1998), 9.

2. Article by Richard C. Leonard, *The Complete Library of Christian Worship,* Vol. 1, Robert Webber, ed. (Nashville, TN: Starsong Publishing Group, 1993), 23.

3. "Holy, Holy, Holy," words by Reginald Heber, music by John B. Dykes. Public domain.

4. "You Are Lord of Heaven" by David Morris. Copyright © 1986 Integrity's Hosanna! Music/ASCAP. All rights reserved. International copyright secured. Used by permission. C/O Integrity Music, Inc., 1000 Cody Road, Mobile, AL 36695.

5. Richard Montez, "My Search for Jesus," via Internet (Dallas, TX: April 5, 2001).

6. Judson Cornwall, *Let Us Worship* (Gainesville, FL: Bridge-Logos Publishing, 1983).

Chapter 2
The Father Is Seeking Worshipers

1. "I Am Thine, O Lord," words by Fanny J. Crosby, music by William H. Doane. Public domain.

2. "Worshipers of You" by Andrea Schmaltz. Copyright © 2001 Shiloh Music. Contact info: shiloh-music.com.

Chapter 3
Personal Worship and Private Devotion

1. Gary Wiens, "The Beauty of His Holiness," from a Worship Conference at Camphill, Pennsylvania, March 2001.

2. "Near to the Heart of God" by Cleland McAfee. Public domain.

3. David Morris, *A Lifestyle of Worship* (Ventura, CA: Regal Books, 1998), 42.

4. "As the Deer" by Martin J. Nystrom. Copyright © 1984 Maranatha! Praise Inc. Admin. by The Copyright Company. All rights reserved. Used by permission.

Chapter 4
Praise Is...?

1. "Rejoice, the Lord Is King," words by Charles Wesley, music by John Darwall. Public domain.

2. James Strong, *Strong's Exhaustive Concordance* (Nashville, TN.: Crusade Bible Publishers, 1983), 8426.

3. Ibid., 7623.

4. Ibid., 3034.

5. Ibid., 2167.

6. Ibid., 1984.

7. Ibid., 1288.

8. Ibid., 7812.

9. Ibid., 4352.

10. Ibid., 8416.

11. Ibid., 7891.

12. Ibid., 7540.

13. Ibid., 7442.

14. "Clap Your Hands" by Bob Kauflin. Copyright © 1986 Integrity's Praise! Music/BMI & PDI Praise/BMI (admin. by Integrity's Praise! Music/BMI). All rights reserved. International Copyright secured. Used by permission. C/O Integrity Music, Inc., 1000 Cody Road, Mobile, AL 36695.

Chapter 5
The Dynamics of Corporate Worship

1. George W. Barna, "The Pastor's Weekly Briefing," quoted by H. B. London, Jr. (Colorado Springs, CO: Focus on the Family Pastoral Ministries).

2. Charles R. Swindoll, *Improving Your Serve* (Dallas, TX: Word Publishing, 1981).

3. Graham Kendrick, "Introducing the March for Jesus," from an address to worship leaders, Dallas, Texas, July 1991.

4. "Blest Be the Tie," words by John Fawcett, music by Johann G. Nageli. Public domain.

5. Article by Ralph Martin, *The Complete Library of Christian Worship*, 259.

6. Bob Sorge, *Exploring Worship* (Canandaigua, NT: Oasis House Publishing, 1987), 136–137.

7. Martin, *The Complete Library of Christian Worship*, 259.

8. Strong, *Strong's Exhaustive Concordance*, 5603.

9. Article by Janice C. Leonard, *The Complete Library of Christian Worship*, 274.

10. "Rise Up" by Randy Fahrendholz. Copyright © 1999, PlayforHim Music. Used by permission.

Chapter 6
The Table of the Lord

1. "Let Us Break Bread Together," words and music a Negro spiritual. Public domain.

2. "Here Is Bread, Here Is Wine" by Graham Kendrick. Copyright © 1991 Make Way Music, admin. by Music Services. All rights reserved. Used by permission.

Chapter 7
Playing Skillfully

1. Reverend J., *"Sacred vs. secular Music,"* via Internet, March 6, 2001.

2. "Psalm 150—Let Everything That Hath Breath," author unknown. Public domain.

3. "With One Voice" by Paul Baloche and Ed Kerr. Copyright © 1995 Integrity's Hosanna! Music/ASCAP. All rights reserved. International copyright secured. Used by permission. C/O Integrity Music, Inc., 1000 Cody Road, Mobile, AL 36695.

Chapter 8
Spiritual Gifts, Intercession and Worship

1. *The Book of Common Prayer—Episcopal* (Kingsport, TN: Kingsport Press, for Church Hymnal Corp., 1977), 52–53.

2. Morris, *A Lifestyle of Worship,* 152–153.

3. John Piper, *Let The Nations Be Glad* (Grand Rapids, MI: Baker Books, 1996), 11.

4. "God of Grace and God of Glory," words by Harry Emerson Fosdick, music by John Hughes. Public domain.

5. Dietrich Bonhoeffer, *Psalms: The Prayer Book of the Bible* (Minneapolis, MN: Augsburg Fortress Publishers, 1974), 14–15.

6. Morris, *A Lifestyle of Worship,* 123–124.

7. "Salvation" by Charlie Hall, copyright © 2000, Six Steps Music/worshiptogether.com. Admin. by Music Services. All rights reserved. Used by permission.

8. Judson Cornwall, *The Philosophy of Worship* (Columbus, GA: Christian Life Publications, 1998), 98.

Chapter 9
Worship and Warfare—Scattering His Enemies

1. "A Mighty Fortress" by Martin Luther. Public domain.

2. David Blomgren, *Restoring Praise and Worship to the Church* (Shippensburg, PA: Revival Press, 1989), 76.

3. "Our God" by Dean Mitchum. Copyright © 1997, Christian International Music. All rights reserved. Used by permission.

4. Morris, *A Lifestyle of Worship,* 144–145.

Chapter 10
One River—Many Streams of Worship

1. Craig Brian Larson, *Illustrations for Preaching and Teaching* (Grand Rapids, MI: Baker Books, 1993), 179.

2. Barna, "The Pastor's Weekly Briefing."

3. "O Church of God, United," words by Frederick B. Morley. Copyright © 1954, renewed 1982 by The Hymn Society. Admin. by Hope Publishing Co., Carol Stream, IL 60188. All rights reserved. Used by permission.

4. *The Complete Library of Christian Worship,* 222.

5. LaMar Boschman, *Future Worship* (Ventura, CA: Renew Books, 1999), 139.

6. T. P. Carter, *Jokes, Notes and Quotes* (Columbus, GA: Quill Publications, 1991), 135.

7. Andy Park, "Worship Is a Lifestyle," *Voice of the Vineyard Magazine* (Fall 1997): 14.

8. "All Over the World" by Terry Butler. Copyright © 1995, Mercy/Vineyard Publishing (ASCAP), admin. by Music Services. All rights reserved. Used by permission.

A Totally Practical, Non-Religious Guide to Understanding Your Christian Faith

YOUR JOURNEY STARTS HERE with this **bold, convicting, non-judgmental, thought-provoking, one-of-a-kind Journey of Faith series.** Each interactive study draws you closer to God's heart where you will find grace and mercy without feeling condemned or overwhelmed. Every page offers you an opportunity to discover an exciting eternal relationship that can grow and go with you for the rest of your life. Take the first step and start your journey here...

ENJOYING YOUR JOURNEY WITH GOD

BY DANIEL BROWN, PH.D.
God delights in you, loves you—and even likes you! It's time to move away from religion and into a relationship with God. You can encounter and examine God close up, through biblical eyes.

CALLED TO RADICAL DEVOTION BY DAVID MORRIS

Get ready for a discovery that will shatter all your myths and misconceptions about worship!

DRAWING CLOSER TO GOD'S HEART BY EDDIE AND ALICE SMITH

Do you know what concerns are on God's heart?

Plugged Into God's Power BY DOUG BEACHAM

Explore a non-religious teaching on an extremely spiritual subject. **Coming in March 2002**

These totally practical guides to understanding different aspects of your Christian faith are ideal for individual study, small group study, leadership training and Sunday school. Start your journey today!

Call Today! 1-800-599-5750

Or visit your local Christian bookstore
www.charismawarehouse.com

Charisma HOUSE
Books about Spirit-Led Living

A part of
STRANG
COMMUNICATIONS COMPANY